Critical Thinking Across the Curriculum

Critical Thinking Across the Curriculum

Developing critical thinking skills, literacy and philosophy in the primary classroom

Mal Leicester and Denise Taylor

Open University Press

Open University Press
McGraw-Hill Education
McGraw-Hill House
Shoppenhangers Road
Maidenhead
Berkshire
England
SL6 2QL

email: enquiries@openup.co.uk
world wide web: www.openup.co.uk

and Two Penn Plaza, New York, NY 10121-2289, USA

First published 2010
Reprinted 2010

A catalogue record of this book is available from the British Library

ISBN-13: 978-0-33-523879-8 (pb)
ISBN-10: 0335238793 (pb)

Library of Congress Cataloging-in-Publication Data
CIP data applied for

Typeset by RefineCatch Limited, Bungay, Suffolk
Printed in the UK by Ashford Colour Press Ltd., Gosport, Hants.

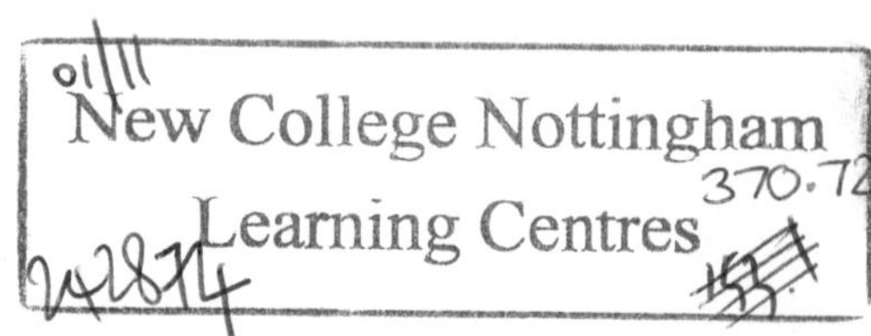

The McGraw-Hill Companies

Contents

List of Stories/Illustrations

Photocopiable Resources

Acknowledgements

We would like to thank Mikaela Revell, Charlotte Taylor and Aidan Dover for demonstrating perfectly the critical thinking skills through their Learning to Cook activities in Chapter 9.

It has been a pleasure working with our editor Monika Lee on this project. Having worked with her previously, we have found Monika to be very supportive, and gently but firmly encouraging on deadlines and improvements.

We are grateful to Taryn Shrigley-Wightman for her illustrations which add another dimension to this book and others.

Denise Taylor would like to thank Mal Leicester for her invitation to co-author on this book. Mal has long been a great mentor to me, a constant source of inspiration, and through this project has helped me increase my own knowledge on critical thinking issues.

Introduction

Story and Critical Thinking

In our recent book, *Environmental Learning for Classroom and Assembly at KS1 and KS2* (Leicester and Taylor 2009), we combined the power of story with the magic of nature. In this book, once more we use the power of story, this time to explore the different aspects of critical thinking. Each story embodies one of the critical thinking concepts, making complex and abstract ideas concrete and accessible.

Philosophers and others who think about highly abstract ideas have often used story in this way. For example, the question of God's existence has been explored using the metaphor of a beautiful garden discovered in natural woodland. Its order and design suggest the existence of a gardener who has created and nurtured it. Or, could it have grown like this just by chance, as distinct from through deliberate planning?

By taking abstract ideas, philosophical questions and critical skills as central themes in thought-provoking children's stories, we introduce relevant concepts in a way children will readily understand and will also enjoy.

The Nature of Critical Thinking

We have organized critical thinking skills into two main categories. In Part 1, we explore various aspects of critical reflection at levels appropriate to KS1 and KS2. These aspects include: asking good questions, understanding point of view, being rational, and developing the skills of research and of analysis. In Part 2 we introduce children to philosophical reflection and explore the nature of knowledge, moral dilemmas and the problem of perception.

Each chapter begins with an explanation of that chapter's critical skill and explores this in a way that will be understood by primary school children. In this way we comprehensively cover relevant concepts (reason, evidence, logical consistency and contradiction, analysis, values, knowledge, philosophy etc.). The chapters' learning activities develop the concepts associated with the skills (recognizing assumptions and bias, imagining alternatives, using evidence and logic, learning to be reflective), and provide practice in relevant thought processes and tools (asking good questions, giving good reasons, categorizing material etc.). We have divided these learning activities into KS1 and KS2 levels. However, most teachers will find both sets of activities appropriate for some of their children, and, suitably adapted, for the whole class.

Critical thinking can be thought of as a toolbox of skills which enable children to think more deeply and clearly about what they believe (and what they read or are told in the media etc.), and about what they should do. Such thinking will help them to be better informed and less open to biased persuasion, to prejudice and to irrational behaviour or belief. It is important that children develop these skills in school because learning how to be critical and how to think for oneself are key elements in becoming educated. For teachers who want to develop their own critical thinking, in a recent book by Mal Leicester, *Teaching Critical Thinking Skills* (2010, Continuum), critical thinking concepts and skills are explored at an adult level with adult stories to embody key ideas.

Critical Thinking and the Curriculum: Cross-curricular Concerns

Since the publication of the *Independent Review of the Primary Curriculum: Final Report* (DCSF 2009) there has been a renewed emphasis on cross-curricular learning in the primary classroom. This book will be a useful resource for encouraging such cross-curricular work. It will provide cross-curricular understanding in three ways:

- **Literacy**

  The skills of listening, speaking (oral communication), reading and writing are cross-curricular. In each chapter the story and the associated learning activities promote all aspects of the children's literacy.

- **Values education**

  Values also cross the curriculum and the national curriculum recognizes and requires that teachers have regard to the children's personal, social, moral, cultural and spiritual development. Because stories necessarily embody core human values, they and the stories' activities will contribute to values education.

- **Critical and creative thinking skills**

  The skills of critical thinking also cross the entire curriculum. In all areas of human knowledge and understanding we need to learn to be critical – questioning, reflective, rational etc. Thus these skills could be said to be generic, though they take different forms in the different areas. For example, a questioning habit will help to initiate children into all areas of knowledge and is thus an essential cross-curricular tool. However, what counts as a good question varies from domain to domain and the children need to grasp these differences. The critical thinking learning activities (the exercises and games) include subject-specific and more generic work.

  Moreover, critical and creative thinking overlap. For example, the critical thinking aspect of 'imagining alternatives' is also an exercise in creativity. Stories are imaginative constructs, which is why they are often described as creative writing. Thus the story, activities and the critical thinking exercises and games provided as key learning in each chapter will help to develop the children's criticality and their creativity.

Interdisciplinary work also crosses the curriculum in the sense that it draws on more than one area of the curriculum in exploring a suitable topic. Such an approach allows staff to pool their various specialist skills. To complete the book's usefulness to cross-curricular approaches, we have provided photographs which link with the chapter stories and concepts and some of these provide a focus for an interdisciplinary project.

How to Use the Book

Used with flexibility the material provided is appropriate for KS1 and KS2. The book provides ten original thought-provoking stories, chapter by chapter explanations of the key critical thinking skills at the appropriate level, lovely illustrations and photographs, and critical thinking learning activities which cross the curriculum and which also practise literacy and creative thinking skills. Photocopiable pages provide ready-made classroom resources for practising all these key, cross-curricular skills.

Each chapter will help you to explain an aspect of critical thinking to your pupils. After the explanation, read the story which follows and which explores this aspect. Deal with difficult vocabulary in your usual way. Now move on to the associated learning activities. For these set a pace which suits you and your class. Both the stories and the activities should set your children thinking in ways that will stimulate their interest as they simultaneously develop their critical and creative skills.

By the end of Chapter 10 the children will understand what it means to be critical and will know how to be so. They will also have been introduced to philosophical and ethical reflection. We hope that they will have become deeper, clearer and more creative thinkers.

PART 1
Aspects of Critical Thinking

CHAPTER

1 Asking Questions

We become critical thinkers gradually. Children learn to become more and more critical in a process which involves practice to improve the habits and tools of critical thought. A central habit is that of **asking questions**. What are the assumptions being made? Are they rational assumptions? What are the hidden or implicit assumptions and values in the claims? How does the context influence the claims? Who is making the claims and why? Are they well supported by good evidence? Are there better alternatives?

The ability to imagine alternatives is often associated with creative thinking. To think 'outside the box' can stimulate both creative and critical thought.

Stephen Brookfield has explored these aspects of critical thinking (Brookfield 1987).

Generalizations based on limited experience can be useful but may also be misleading. Similarly, prejudice is irrational and leads to biased generalizations, often based on stereotypes of the disfavoured group.

Explain to the Children

- Sweeping statements (all X or every Y) are proved wrong by just one exception. '*All swans are white*' was proved wrong as soon as a black swan was discovered. Often we mean 'almost all' rather than 'all', and 'usually' or 'often' rather than 'always'. Children should be wary of all or nothing thinking.
- Not to know, to feel confused or uncertain is often a step to better understanding.
- It is difficult to be open-minded and questioning when our own wants are involved, or our own prejudices. Check with extra care for dubious assumptions and generalizations.
- A table may look small in a large room, and big in a small room. In the same way, context makes a difference in the world of ideas too.
- To imagine different ways of thinking about an idea or a different way of doing something is creative. It can also help us to see the usual way of doing it more clearly and to see the assumptions and limitations, the strengths and weaknesses of the usual way.

The Skills

- The children need to develop the habit of asking questions.
- They need to learn to recognize good questions, and to see the difference between different kinds of questions.
- They need to learn to take account of context. (Note to teacher: To relate a claim or belief to its context helps the development of thinking relativistically – an advanced critical skill.)
- By imagining alternatives they learn that there is often more than one way of thinking about something or doing something.

Preliminaries to the Story and Vocabulary

In the story *Far From Home*, Molly the albatross has strayed off course and found herself a long way from home in a land unfamiliar to her. She is rescued by Judith, a young Ugandan girl on a student exchange in the UK, who is also far from home and in unfamiliar surroundings.

Judith and her new-found friends in the seaside town want to help Molly to return to her home across the Atlantic ocean, but don't know how to do this. This novel and rare situation gives rise to a lot of questions about where the albatross is from, how she came to be so far off course, and what they can do to help her to return home.

The children use a variety of methods for finding the information they need. They seek the help of adults, including experts on birds, and ask them many questions, and they use books and the Internet to find out more about albatrosses.

Vocabulary	
Squawked	cried loudly and harshly – usually a bird
Struggled	fought with an adversary or opposing force
Albatross	a type of large marine bird
Migration	the act of migrating or moving from one place to another
Perplexed	bewildered or puzzled
Thermals	rising air currents caused by the underlying surface
Snuggled	nestled or cuddled
Ornithologist	a scientist who studies birds and their behaviour

Far From Home

Photocopiable Resource

Far From Home

Judith walked slowly along the tide line looking for shells and shiny pebbles. She was concentrating hard, and almost tripped over the bird that was tangled up in a piece of blue nylon fishing net. The bird squawked and struggled to get out of the netting and away from her. She could see that one of its wings had been injured.

'Sssshhhh little bird,' she said softly to it.

She bent down and sat quietly by the bird. After a little while it stopped struggling and looked at her. It had a comical-looking beak which was long and hooked, with a long yellow strip down it. Its eyes were large and black, and watched her cautiously.

Judith had never seen a bird like this before and wondered what it was. She knew it wasn't a seagull. She had seen seagulls all the time on this beach since she arrived here, and this didn't look like any she knew. She took off her coat and gently placed it over the bird and then scooped up the little parcel to carry it home. The bird lay very still in her arms.

'Hello, Judith, what have you there?' Bill, the old fisherman, shouted across to her as she walked past his cabin on the seafront. He was busy cleaning out buckets and tidying his fishing nets.

'It's an injured bird,' Judith called back to him.

'Let's have a look then.'

Judith showed Bill the bird, gently opening up her coat until the bird's head popped out.

'My, my, well I never!' exclaimed Bill. 'It's an albatross. I wonder what it's doing here. You never see birds like that on these shores.'

Judith thought for a moment. *What does he mean? If it wasn't from here, where was it from?* Judith had read about bird migrations, but she couldn't remember reading about albatrosses and where they lived.

Sensing that Judith was a little perplexed, Bill added, 'Albatrosses wander the Atlantic ocean for hundreds, sometimes thousands of miles. They follow the ships looking for food to eat, but then get caught up on the fishing lines, and drown.'

'That's awful,' said Judith, shocked by this news.

'It is,' agreed Bill. 'But it looks like this little one has had a lucky escape. What are you going to do with it now?'

'I don't know,' said Judith. 'I haven't thought about that yet.'

'Tell you what,' said Bill. 'Why don't I look after it for now in the cabin until you decide? I've got some fish scraps it can have, and it will be safe here. I'll take a look at its wing too to make sure it's not too badly injured.'

'That's brilliant. Thanks, Bill,' said Judith, gratefully.

Later Judith met up with her new friends Sam and Harry. They had been helping her to get to know the area since she arrived in England, and they had been really interested in finding out all about Uganda, where she was from.

The three of them went to the local library and spent the afternoon finding out all they could about the albatross. They learned that she was an Atlantic mollymawk, which was also known as a yellow-nosed albatross. They looked up where mollymawks lived, and how they travelled long distances across the Atlantic in search of food, riding high on the thermals so they didn't have to use much energy. They watched videos of albatrosses on the Internet, and laughed when they saw one of an albatross running across the sand dunes trying to take off to fly.

'That looks *so* ridiculous,' laughed Sam. 'How on earth can such a big bird like that take off?'

It was getting late, and before she went home Judith wanted to check on the bird, which they had all agreed should now be called Molly.

We have to think of a way to get Molly home too, she thought to herself. *Perhaps Bill could help us.*

'Well! What did you find out?' asked Bill, when they arrived back at the cabin.

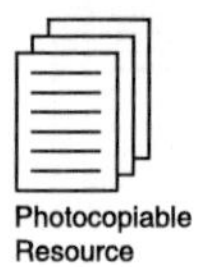

Photocopiable Resource

'She's a mollymawk,' Judith answered. 'And she's a very long way from home. We want to know how we can help to get her back there.'

Bill thought about this for a while. 'Well! We need to know a lot more about our little Molly first. I'll tell you what. Let's ask the experts. The RSPB have a centre at the nature reserve just up the beach from here. I'll give them a ring.'

Dr Chatham, an expert from the RSPB, came to look at Molly the following morning. He brought a camera, a laptop, measuring equipment, and lots of information about marine birds. Judith, Harry and Sam had arrived at Bill's cabin early and were waiting impatiently. Molly looked very settled in and was snuggled up in one of Bill's old fisherman's sweaters.

I bet she likes that sweater so much because it stinks of fish, thought Judith.

Dr Chatham picked Molly up very gently and checked her wings and legs and looked at her beak very closely.

'She appears to be fine, and there's not too much damage done,' he announced. 'She should be able to fly, and she seems strong enough.'

'Will she be able to fly all the way home?' asked Sam.

'I don't think so,' replied Dr Chatham. 'Mollymawks live way out in the middle of the Atlantic ocean.'

'What will happen to her if she can't get back home?' asked Judith, anxiously.

'Well, at this stage, let's see what we can find out about her first. She has a leg ring so I can get some information from that. Someone has put this ring on her so that they can study her, where she flies, what distances she covers, and how long she is away from her nest. That means that there is someone interested in where Molly is, and perhaps they might help to get her back home.'

Judith was cheered up by this news. She had been very worried that Molly might have to go to a zoo and be put in a cage, and in her heart she knew that this was not the right thing for an albatross that was used to flying free across the oceans.

'Can you show me where you found her, Judith?' asked Dr Chatham. 'I need to record the information for our records. And no doubt the local newspaper will be interested too. This is such an amazing adventure for Molly, and I think we've only ever had one other case of an albatross in the UK before.'

Judith showed Dr Chatham where she had found Molly, and the fishing line that she had been caught up in. He took some photographs, and afterwards went back to the nature reserve to make some phone calls and to check the information on Molly's leg ring.

The next day he returned to Bill's cabin.

'I've got some good news,' he announced to the children. 'Yesterday I did quite a bit of research, and managed to find the ornithologists who put the ring on Molly's leg. They're going to arrange for her to be transported back to her island nest next week.'

'That's great news,' said Bill. 'The wanderer returns,' he chuckled.

'Very funny, Bill!' said Judith. 'But we all know that Molly isn't a wandering albatross. She's a mollymawk. We checked, remember.'

'That's right, you did,' laughed Bill. 'I should learn to get my facts right, eh kids?'

Talking About the Story

Ask the Children

- Why was Molly far from home?
- How had Molly been injured?
- What type of bird was Molly?
- How did the children find out what type of bird Molly was?
- Which country was Judith from?
- Why was Judith worried about Molly being put in a zoo?

Points for Discussion

- The children in the story find out about the mollymawk by asking questions and obtaining information. Discuss with the children the different sources of information (for example, books, the Internet, asking other people, asking experts, watching videos, etc.).
- There are different kinds of questions such as primary and secondary questions, where the original question leads on to further questions about the subject. There are also questions that are factual (which have only one correct answer), interpretive (have more than one answer but which must still be supported by evidence) or evaluative (questions that ask for an opinion or point of view).
- The different subjects the children study in school (the National Curriculum) also produce their own kind of questions. Discuss with the children scientific questions, aesthetic questions (art), historical questions, etc. Can they produce questions for each of these domains?

Cross-curricular Story Activities

Key Stage 1 Activity

Ask the children if anyone has been to another country or a different town. Where was it? What was it like? After this discussion, ask the children to draw or paint their own picture about being far from home. They could imagine a scene on a beach in another country, like the story. Or they could imagine being in a foreign village or town. What does a strange land look like? What are the houses like? What do the people look like? The strange land could be another planet and they could draw or paint weird and wonderful creatures. Or being far from home could mean being in a different time either long ago or far into the future, for example ancient Egypt or Stone Age Britain.

Key Stage 2 Activity

The Rhyme of the Ancient Mariner is about an albatross. Read the poem to the children and then ask them to write their own poem or story about an albatross and the journey it makes. Alternatively, they could write a story or poem about a long journey they have made or one they would like to make.

For Enthusiastic or Gifted Children

In the story, the mollymawk landing so far from home was a rare occurrence. There are many reasons why this could have happened, and deeper and more searching questions could be asked about cause and effect (see Chapter 3). For example, changes in global weather systems disrupt the migration patterns of birds. The children could carry out further research to find out more about albatrosses and how weather systems and fishing practices affect their population numbers.

Critical Thinking Activities

Key Stage 1 Activities

KS1 Activity 1: Guessing Games

Guessing games are a good way of developing questioning skills in younger children. There are a number of games the children will enjoy, as a whole class or in small groups. One simple game is to collect pictures of different animals, or different objects. The object of the game is that one person in the group chooses an animal or object without revealing its identity to the rest of the group or class. The children take turns asking questions to try and identify the animal or object. To make the game harder you can limit the number of questions that can be asked in a time period.

After the game has finished, discuss with the children the different types of questions they used. Did they use open or closed questions, factual questions, etc? Which types of questions obtained more information?

KS1 Activity 2: Asking Question

Give the children a copy of the photograph *Man and Two Birds* (*Photocopiable Resource 1*) on page 17. Read the questions to the children and write a selection of their answers on the whiteboard. If there is time, the children could think of some more questions of their own about the picture.

Key Stage 2 Activities

KS2 Activity 1: Open and Closed Questions

Give the children a copy of Rudyard Kipling's poem (*Photocopiable Resource 3*) on page 19. Discuss the differences between open and closed questions. Divide the children into groups and give each group two objects. One is an everyday object such as a pen or a ruler and the other is an unusual object such as a shell or a fossil. Working in their groups, the children use the open and closed questions to find out as much as they can about the objects. Discuss with the children how much information they managed to find about the everyday object and how much information about the unusual object. Which type of questions did they use? Which questions provided them with the most information? When did they use open questions? When did they use closed questions? What were the results?

KS2 Activity 2: Role Play

Divide the class into groups, and explain that they are going to take turns at being a journalist or reporter. As reporters the children will interview their classmates about an event in their life that they are going to write about for the school magazine. Ask the children who are being interviewed to think of a holiday, or a memorable event in their life, or a hobby they enjoy.

Allow ten minutes for each interview, with children taking turns, and then allow a further twenty minutes for them to write up their report.

Remind the children about asking open questions to obtain the most information from their interviewees.

For Enthusiastic or Gifted Children

Enthusiastic or gifted children could look at and evaluate articles from local newspapers, paying attention to the structure of the article, and the way the sentences have been structured.

Photocopiable Resource 1

Man and Two Birds

Photocopiable Resource 2

Questions for the photograph Man and Two Birds *in Resource 1*

1. Why are there people dressed in bird costumes?

2. What do you think they are saying to the man in the picture?

3. Why do you think the man in the picture is looking so surprised?

4. What event do you think they are at?

Photocopiable Resource 3

I Keep Six Honest Serving-Men ...

(from *The Elephant's Child's* story by Rudyard Kipling, *Just So Stories*, p. 75)

I keep six honest serving-men
(They taught me all I knew);
Their names are What and Why and When
And How and Where and Who.
I send them over land and sea,
I send them east and west;
But after they have worked for me,
I give them all a rest.

I let them rest from nine till five,
For I am busy then,
As well as breakfast, lunch, and tea,
For they are hungry men.
But different folk have different views;
I know a person small –
She keeps ten million serving-men,
Who get no rest at all!

She sends 'em abroad on her own affairs,
From the second she opens her eyes –
One million Hows, two million Wheres,
And seven million Whys!

CHAPTER

2 Point of View

Forming Your Own Point of View

It is not rational to take on a ready-made **point of view**. We need to think about these to make sure we have good reasons for that point of view. Thus, to be a critical thinker involves reflecting on our own beliefs and viewpoints. Teachers rightly want their pupils to form opinions of their own and to develop independent thought. This goes with the child developing self-confidence as well as criticality.

Children need to learn to evaluate evidence and assess how provisionally a belief **deserves** to be held. To hold a belief provisionally is not an inability to form an opinion, but to recognize that we have different degrees and kinds of evidence for our different beliefs.

Different Points of View

Changing one's point of view is, in a way, another form of exploring alternatives. Reading and writing stories helps us to experience the different points of view of the characters.

Explain to the Children

- A questioning attitude means paying attention to assumptions, reasoning and evidence informing your own point of view.
- Your point of view should be your **own** – worked out by you and not just copied from someone else.
- Think about whether your point of view matches your experience and whether you can develop or improve your point of view.
- Different people have different experiences and develop different points of view.
- To understand other people (in real life or in a story) try to understand their experience and their viewpoint. Similarly, to even understand other non-human creatures, it helps if we can try to understand their experiences – their needs and wants.

The Skills

- The children need to be able to give reasons for their point of view.
- They need to develop empathy – the ability to understand other people's experience and point of view. (Stories help with the development of this kind of understanding.)

Preliminaries to the Story and Vocabulary

In this story, the children find a piece of rock with a fluorescent glow inside it. The rock acts like a prism and, when viewed from different angles, the light appears to be a different colour or shape. Each child has their own idea or point of view about what the light represents.

How we perceive events in our lives is shaped by our social and cultural experiences, which can also act as filters when forming our own opinions. In addition, we use our past experiences and our beliefs as reference points when we encounter something new or novel. The children in the story each have a different idea about what the light is, which is influenced by their own past experiences.

Light can be distorted, refracted, reflected and diffused, and this is a good example to use when explaining to children how our assumptions and beliefs can also be distorted and diffused by our different cultural and social filters and influences. Forming our own opinions requires us to question underlying assumptions and to search for evidence, or to use logic, to help us to arrive at the truth.

Vocabulary	
Exploring	going on a journey of discovery
Stalagmite	a deposit, usually of calcium carbonate, from constantly dripping water which forms a column on the floor of a cave
Stalactite	a deposit, usually of calcium carbonate, from constantly dripping water which forms an icicle shape from the roof of a cave
Slippery	tending to cause slipping or sliding often caused by ice, oil or water on a flat surface
Cavern	a large cave, usually underground
Echo	repetition of a sound being reflected back from a hard surface such as a wall, or mountainside in a valley
Shimmer	light that appears to quiver or vibrate
Translucent	allowing light to pass through but diffusing it so that the object is not totally clear
Galaxy	a large system of stars held together by mutual gravitation

Genie	a spirit, that appears in human form when summoned
Fluorite	a common mineral, calcium fluoride, occurring in green, blue, purple, yellow or colourless crystals
Geology	the science that deals with the dynamics and physical history of the Earth, and the rocks it is composed of
Flourish	make dramatic sweeping gestures

The Blue John Star Lantern

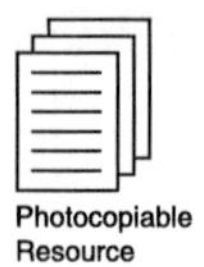
Photocopiable Resource

The Blue John Star Lantern

Malik was on a school trip with his best friends. They were exploring the Blue John mine in the Peak District as part of their geography lessons. They were supposed to be learning about stalagmites and stalactites, but Malik was bored by this and wanted to do something much more exciting. His friends all seemed to be having great fun leaning over a barrier and dropping tiny stones down a deep shaft, listening for the sound of them hitting the bottom, but he didn't want to do that. He wanted to go exploring.

Just above him Malik could see an opening to a tunnel. There was a small ledge and some large boulders. A rope barrier had been placed in front of the ledge with a sign that said 'No Entry'. Malik could see that the rest of the school group had already moved on, leaving him and his friends behind.

'Hey, you guys, let's explore this tunnel,' Malik called across to his friends.

Georgie wasn't too sure. She looked at the sign and said, 'It's too dangerous, Malik. We'll get into trouble.'

But Ben and Lucy wanted an adventure too, and agreed with Malik. Mai, who was the shyest member of the gang, always went along with whatever the others decided, and so it wasn't long before they climbed over the barrier and scrambled up on to the ledge.

Inside the tunnel, the floor was cold and slippery. It sloped upwards for a while before widening out. It was very dark, but Lucy, who was a Brownie, had come prepared. She had brought a head torch with her, and they shone it into the tunnel.

The tunnel opened out into a large cavern. They couldn't see all of it in the gloom, and so they decided to stay close to the wall and follow it round to see how big it was. Their voices echoed all around them. Lucy shone the torch to light up the cave wall ahead of them.

'What's that?' said Ben, excitedly. 'Look! There's a light.'

A faint glow shimmered in the darkness. Being the most daring and adventurous of the group, Malik walked towards the glow. The others followed him hesitantly.

'Isn't this the Witch's Hall?' said Ben, mischievously.

'Whoooooo oooooo,' he moaned in his best ghostly voice.

'You're not frightening us, so just shut up,' said Georgie, who was feeling a little bit scared. She didn't like the dark, and the strange light made her nervous.

'It's OK,' said Malik. 'It's just a rock that glows in the dark. Come and see.'

Malik picked up the rock. It was a purply-blue coloured crystal with yellow streaks. It was translucent, and its sides were all different shapes and sizes. In the middle a tiny light glowed brightly.

'It's like a little lantern,' said Malik, handing the rock crystal to Lucy.

'Wow!' she exclaimed. 'It's beautiful. If you look really closely and screw up your eyes, it looks like a tiny star in a far away galaxy.'

The others passed the rock to each other, and studied it carefully from different angles. The light pulsed and shimmered a little more brightly as the rock was turned over and over in their hands.

'We must be in Witch's Cave,' said Mai. 'I think it's a magic spell that has been trapped in there.'

'I think it's a tiny ghost, like a genie in the lamp in Aladdin,' said Georgie. She rubbed the rock with the sleeve of her coat. The light continued to glow, but no genie appeared.

'No three wishes for us, then,' laughed Ben. 'And anyway, you're all wrong. Give it here.' He took the rock from Georgie. 'See, it's just a rock with some fluorite in it.' Ben wanted to be a scientist when he was older, and had read books about gems, rocks and geology.

'Well, I think my idea of starlight is the best one,' huffed Lucy. 'So, I think we should call it a star lantern, because that's exactly what it looks like.'

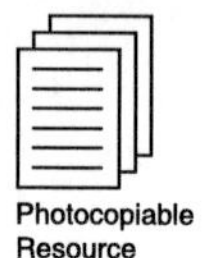
Photocopiable Resource

Suddenly, they heard voices from the next cavern echoing through the tunnel.

'We'd better get back or we'll be in trouble,' said Georgie worriedly.

They hurriedly put the rock into Malik's rucksack, and clambered back through the tunnel to join the rest of their class.

In class the next day their teacher, Miss Leigh, announced that they were to have a whole lesson about their experiences in the Blue John mine, and that everyone should write a story which they would read out to the rest of the class at Show and Tell time. She said the children could work in small groups if they liked.

Malik, Ben, Mai, Georgie and Lucy worked together on their story. They argued for a while about what the light really was, but they all liked the idea of starlight from a distant galaxy being trapped in the rock and decided to call their story *The Star Lantern.*

After reading their story to the rest of the class, Malik slowly opened his rucksack, and then pulled out the rock with a great flourish. 'Da, da,' he cried triumphantly, and held up the rock for everyone to see. He heard a sly giggle from the back of the class. He looked up at the rock as he held it aloft, and couldn't believe his eyes. The light had gone!

Miss Leigh, seeing his disappointment, quickly said: 'That was a wonderful story, and you clearly had a very magical time in the cave. Well done all of you.'

'But, Miss . . .' Malik began to protest. He felt Lucy put a hand on his shoulder. She leant towards him and whispered in his ear.

'Stars don't come out in the daytime, silly.' She winked at him.

The others heard her and smiled. She was right.

Talking About the Story

Ask the Children

- What were Malik's friends doing at the beginning of the story?
- What are stalagmites and stalactites?
- What was the cave called that they went into?
- What did the children discover in the cave?
- Why was Georgie nervous about the light?
- Who thought the rock was a star in a far away galaxy?
- What did the children call their own story about the light in the rock?
- Why did the light in the rock not shine at the end of the story?

Points for Discussion

- The rock that the children found contained fluorite which can release light when exposed to ultra-violet light. Some fluorites can also emit light when coming into contact with heat in a process called thermoluminescence. Because the children did not know what was causing the light, they used their own experiences and creative thinking to arrive at possible conclusions. Ask the children what they think made the rock glow? Can they think of some other explanations?
- In the story, the characters each have their own idea about what the light in the rock crystal is. Discuss each point of view with the children and explore the assumptions of each character. For example, Mai though the rock contained a ghost because they were in the Witch's Cave. Ben thought the rock was fluorite because he had read about fluorite. This is an assumption based on scientific knowledge as distinct from the creative imagination. This assumption gives the correct explanation. Scientific knowledge is wonderful too!

Cross-curricular Story Activities

Key Stage 1 Activities

1. Let the children experience different points of view by pretending to be different creatures using colourful masks.
2. Photocopy the two animal masks (*Photocopiable Resources 6 and 7*) on pages 33 and 34 onto thick card and ask the children to colour in or paint them. For additional masks the children could draw and paint their own animal

masks or even masks depicting imaginary creatures. Thread the masks with string, wool or ribbon so that the children can wear the masks. Ask the children to imagine they are the creature their mask represents. How does it behave? What noises does it make?

3. Allow some free play time in a large open space where the children can run around pretending to be their chosen creature, and can also take turns swapping their masks and pretending to be other creatures.

Key Stage 2 Activities

1. KS2 children could do the mask activity described above for KS1. Additionally they could write a short piece about their experience as the different creatures, and how they felt.
2. Explain to the children that stories are written using a narrative point of view which can be in the first or third person. Let the children write a short piece first of all in the first person, and then the same piece in the third person. Discuss with the children how the different characters feel.
3. Use the theme of the story about the star lantern and the photograph of *Moonlight Reflection on Lake* (*Photocopiable Resource 4*) on page 31 to encourage creative thinking about the different sources of light.
4. Ask the children to imagine they are the sun, the moon, or a distant star. Each wants to be the brightest one to light up the Earth, and competes with the others.

Encourage the children to think about:

- The brightness of their own light.
- Does it make the trees and flowers grow?
- Does it warm the Earth? Or is it a cold light?
- What colour is the light? Is it many different colours?
- What can they see when their light shines down on the Earth?
- What effect does the light have on the Earth, its people and all the plants and animals?

For Enthusiastic or Gifted Children

There is a rich resource in literature about the sun, the moon and the stars. The children could carry out further research using the Internet or the library to explore stories, poems and songs on this subject. Ask them to select their favourites and then work with the children to explore the different points of view of the authors and the points of view of the subject.

Critical Thinking Activities

Key Stage 1 Activity

KS1 Activity 1: Optical Illusions

Using the Internet, obtain a number of different examples of optical illusions. Ask the children to describe what they see. Some illusions have a subject that could be either one thing or another, such as the well-known duck/rabbit illusion on page 32 (*Photocopiable Resource 5*). Use the illusions to open up discussion about how easy it is for us to see something and believe it to be one thing when, in fact, there is more to it than meets the eye. The aim of this exercise is to encourage the children to question what it is they are actually seeing and what assumptions they are making.

(Note to teacher: The great philosopher, Wittgenstein, uses the duck/rabbit illustration in his *Philosophical Investigations* (1953)).

This duck/rabbit illustration is clearly relevant to the problem of perception discussed in Chapter 10.

Key Stage 2 Activities

KS2 Activity 1: Predator and Prey Role Play Game

This activity works better when played outdoors, ideally in a green space, but the playground will work just as well.

Role play is an excellent way to demonstrate point of view, and there are numerous scenarios or situations that can be used. Children can take turns in playing the different roles, and exploring the different points of view.

Divide the children into groups of at least six people. In each group two of the children will play the role of predators (e.g. wolves, bears, foxes, birds of prey). The rest of the group will play the role of prey (e.g. rabbits, deer, small birds).

Mark off two or three areas that can be used as 'safe places' where the prey can 'hide' from the predators. These should be placed sufficiently wide apart that the prey animals have to run some distance before they reach another safe place, thus giving the predators an opportunity to catch them. The prey animals are only allowed to stay on the safe places for a count of 30 seconds before they have to move off.

Allow the children ten minutes per session. The object is for the predators to capture as many prey species as they can. If they capture a prey animal, then that child is out of the game.

To start the game, the prey species could start on a safe place, and the predators should be at the edge of the play area, and not too close to the safe places.

Assign two or three children in the class to keep a tally of the scores, and to keep a track of the time.

Allow time to discuss the different points of view after the game has taken place, and to explore the assumptions and beliefs with the whole class. Ask the children to write about their experience. Was it harder being a predator or a prey animal?

KS2 Activity 2: Developing Empathy

Choose a well-known story or fairytale with characters that the children can strongly identify with and with whom they can feel empathy. The hero or heroine may have had a bad experience or a particular triumph. Discuss the feelings and motivations of the character or characters with the children. Do they feel the same as the hero or heroine, or would they have taken another course of action? What if the hero or heroine did something completely opposite to what is portrayed in the story? What would the likely outcomes be?

This exercise will help the children to understand other people's point of view that may be different from their own.

For Enthusiastic or Gifted Children

Older KS2 children could explore examples of media manipulation, where what is being portrayed in a press photograph is not what actually happened. Such manipulation usually occurs when there are two opposing views, and the power of imagery and words has been used to convey a story that is not what it seems. If appropriate, discuss the concepts of propaganda and indoctrination.

(Also, see Critical Thinking Activity for KS2 in Chapter 5 about the persuasive power of advertising.)

Photocopiable Resource 4

Moonlight Reflection on Lake

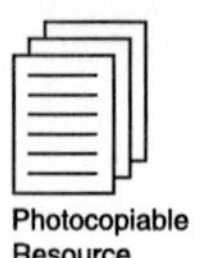

Photocopiable Resource 5

Duck/Rabbit

Photocopiable Resource 6

Tiger Mask

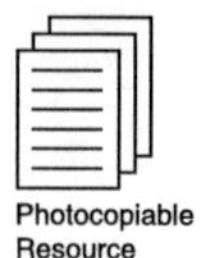

Photocopiable Resource 7

Owl Mask

Interdisciplinary Project

Science

In the story, the rock crystal acts like a prism. Children enjoy working with light and prisms and it can help them to understand how light can refract and bend.

This exercise will help children to understand that light from the sun is made up of a mixture of many different colours of light, even though to the eye the light looks almost white.

Ask the children to think of other things that give off or reflect light and which have a different mix of colours. For example, rain drops can act like prisms.

There are a number of experiments the children could conduct using prisms, a convex lens, a strong light (a torch light or projector light), and a piece of white paper. Ask the children to write down their predictions about how they would have to arrange the objects in order to make the strongest rainbow appear. Then use the objects to test their predictions. Discuss the predictions with the children. Were they right or wrong? What could they have done differently?

Using both rectangular and triangular prisms, ask the children to look at different things through the prisms. For example, they could look at text in a book, or a picture. Ask them to tilt the prisms and look at the objects again. What effect does this have? How does the prism change the shape of things? Does it change the colour? Encourage the children to brainstorm explanations for why the refraction of light caused by the prism might make the text appear different when viewed through each prism.

Art

A number of different art projects could be completed by the children using the themes of rock crystals and/or light.

Explore different materials that reflect, refract or distort light. A simple art activity is to create a stained glass window using different coloured translucent paper (some sweet wrappers are perfect for this).

Obtain some clear rock crystals, and thin nylon or wire, and create miniature window displays or mobiles. These work in the same as the prisms above, and cast interesting coloured shapes and patterns into the room.

Geography and History

The study of geology is interdisciplinary with both geography and history. Children are fascinated by times past, and rock formations provide an insight into different geological eras. The Blue John stone in the story was formed millions of years ago, and Derbyshire is the only place in the world where this particular rock formation is found. This could be used as an example for activities in geography on places where different gems and precious stones can be found throughout the world.

The children could perhaps do some topic work on the world's largest caves and caverns and the treasures found there.

CHAPTER

3 Being Rational

The Concepts

This chapter is about the concepts relating to rational thought. We are rational when we have good reasons for what we do or believe; **reasons** based on **evidence** and **logic**. We need to encourage the children to **justify** their claims by giving good reasons and sound arguments. This, in turn, requires them to recognize strong and weak reasons/evidence and to recognize logical (consistent) arguments and illogical (for example, contradictory) statements.

Evidence

The scientific method is based on observation and experiment. It proceeds by disproving hypotheses through observation and measurement of phenomena in the world. Such evidence is called empirical, depending on trial or experiment, and thus rooted in experience of the real world of objects existing in time and space. One could say that scientific evidence is the most rigorous form of evidence.

Children can begin to understand that we know things through our senses (what we see, hear, taste, smell, touch). Our observation of the world is how we learn about it. What we experience is the bedrock of knowledge, our own knowledge/experience, and it is also the bedrock of the scientific method.

Logic and Sequence

Formal logic is a symbolic system with rules for moving from premises to valid conclusions. However, even if we have not studied formal logic we have a grasp, using ordinary language, of valid and invalid deductions. We need to cultivate this awareness of consistency and contradiction in our pupils. Consistency between statements tends to support a set of beliefs.

Critical thinking will seek order or structure. In other words it will proceed in logical sequences of various kinds.

Explain to the Children

- A reason supports a belief.
- The support comes from good evidence and sensible arguments.
- A reason is not a wish or a preference.

I think it will rain tomorrow because the weather forecast is for rain (reason based on evidence).

I think it will not rain tomorrow because we are having a picnic (a wish, not a reason).

I think it will rain tomorrow because I like rain (a preference, not a reason).

Examples of logical arguments:

I think it will rain tomorrow because it usually rains every day in April. It is April now, therefore it will probably rain.

Weather forecasts are usually correct. The weather forecast is for rain, therefore it will probably rain.

The Skills

The children need to learn:

- to justify what they say or do;
- how to justify what they say or do;
- to recognize good or poor evidence;
- to know how to find good evidence;
- to recognize valid or flawed arguments;
- how to construct valid arguments and to criticize flawed ones.

Create a classroom ethos which values rational thought – the giving of reasons and criticism of unsupported or badly supported claims or contradictory arguments. Such criticism is not of the person but of their argument. (It is not **personal**.) The children should gradually acquire and improve the skills associated with rational thought until such a rational approach towards what they are learning becomes a habitual part of their thinking.

Preliminaries to the Story and Vocabulary

Rain Boy is about Joe, a boy who wants to be on the school football team. To be good enough he needs to practise every day during the school summer holiday. On the first day he bursts his football and must somehow get another one. He does this through a bet with his brother about the weather.

The children need to understand that with a weather house the rain side comes out to forecast rain and the sunshine side to show that sunny weather is on the way. Joe's weather house is always wrong! Joe realizes that he can simply reverse what it is telling him to know whether it will soon rain or shine! (This is a logical insight.)

It is important that you distinguish between fact and fiction. In the story weather houses really can predict the weather and Rain Boy can even wink. In real life this is, of course, not the case. However, weather forecasts are a good subject for introducing the idea of reasons based on evidence. Science-based weather forecasts have been getting more reliable as scientists have learned more about weather systems and patterns helped by advances in technology. However, it is still a complex and incompletely understood matter so, even now, such forecasts can be wrong! The weather is also a good topic for interdisciplinary work and we have linked it with the chapter photograph.

Vocabulary

Unceasing	without stopping
Practise	doing something many times to get better at it
Glanced	gave a quick look
Scowling	frowning hard
Forecast	to say what will happen before it does
Predicting	to claim something will happen before it does
Disappeared	vanished
Jubilant	very pleased
Dent	a hollow in something, which damages it
Borrow	use something that belongs to someone else with their permission for a time before giving it back
Lend	let someone borrow something
Retreating	going back
Emerging	coming out

Rain Boy

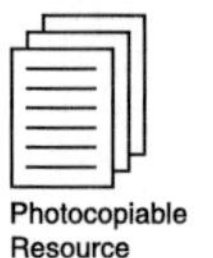
Photocopiable Resource

Rain Boy

I watched the rain rattle against the window, hard as a power shower. Unceasing rain. I sighed deeply.

'We'll practise every day of the holidays,' Lewis had said.

He's already in the school football team and I longed to be picked too. I glanced down at the little weather house on the windowsill. It was wrong as usual. Instead of the scowling Rain Boy, the smiling Sunshine Girl was out.

'I don't know why you keep checking that thing,' said my brother Edward in his know-it-all voice. 'It can't possibly forecast the weather.'

'That's what you think,' I snapped.

'Yes I do think, unlike you,' he said. 'Look at it now, predicting sunshine.'

A little later, however, Sunshine Girl disappeared behind her yellow door and the little black door opened. Rain Boy swung out. *Great,* I thought. *Now the rain will stop.* It did too, and I rushed out of the house to call for Lewis.

'We'll draw posts on the old wall,' he suggested. 'The fields will be too soggy for footie.'

After three hours I was scoring goals every time. Lewis decided to make it more difficult.

'This is the goalie,' he said, standing an old plank against the wall between the chalked posts. 'I'll pass to you Joe and you try to score to one side of the goalie.' He kicked the ball hard and fast and I booted it towards the wall. It thudded against it, exactly half way between the chalked post and the plank.

'Yeah,' we both yelled. We did a jubilant high five.

'We'll keep practising,' Lewis said, 'and you'll make the team in September.' I was smiling as I ran for the ball, but I felt my face fall when I saw it. I'd made a huge dent in its side.

'Oh no,' I said. 'I've not got another one.'

'And we can't use mine either,' said Lewis. 'I lost it at my Nan's. I'll tell you what Joe, borrow Edward's; that lovely one he won.'

'He won't lend it to me,' I said.

'Ask him,' said Lewis, 'otherwise you're stumped. You won't make the team unless we practise every day.'

Back home I thought hard about how I could get a football. Dad was in the garden and I went out to see him.

'Dad,' I said. 'I burst my football and I've got to practise every day!'

'Hard luck, Son,' he said.

'You'd like me to be in the school team wouldn't you Dad?'

He nodded, 'Sure Joe. But if you're after more money, you've had it. You've still not paid me back for that broken window. Remember?'

I went back indoors and tried Mum.

'I need another football, Mum,' I said. 'As soon as possible in fact.'

'Well, I expect you can have one for your birthday, dear,' she said.

'September the fifteenth! I need it now Mum, to practise for making the school team when we go back. Look, tell you what, can I have my birthday early this year, like tomorrow?'

'No Joe, you can't,' said Mum. 'Don't be so silly.'

I felt desperate. There was only Edward left.

'Edward can I borrow yours then?'

Edward hates football, but he had won the ball as a prize for writing a story called *The Beautiful Game*. Mum and I both looked at him. He bit into an apple and slowly chewed it while we waited.

'No way,' he said, at last.

'You know, Edward,' said Mum, 'it's better to be kind than clever.'

'I don't think so,' said Edward.

'Make him lend it, Mum,' I pleaded. 'I'll look after it I promise.'

'I know you would Joe, but I can't lend it to you. It's Edward's ball. It wouldn't be fair. It has to be Edward.'

She sounded sorry, but I felt mad at them both.

* * * * *

I slept badly that night. I knew I could be good enough for the school team but only if I practised. I wasn't quite good enough yet.

Photocopiable Resource

A picture of Edward's prize football came into my mind: its conker-brown leather and tight laces. I thumped my bed in frustration.

Once more I woke to the sound of heavy rain. It matched my mood.

'Even if you had a ball you couldn't play in this,' Edward said.

I glanced down at the weather house. The Sunshine Girl began to retreat behind her yellow door and Rain Boy was slowly emerging from behind his black one.

The weather house was always wrong! That meant ...

'It will be sunny in about ten minutes,' I said.

'I very much doubt it,' said Edward. 'It looks set in for the day.'

He sounded just like a boring adult, and I was just about to yell at him when I had an idea.

'I bet you the use of your ball,' I said.

'What do I get if you're wrong?'

'How about that book voucher. The one I never used.'

'You're on,' said my brother.

We stared out of the window and a few minutes later we saw the rain stop, as suddenly as if a tap had been turned off in the sky. Scowling Edward handed over his ball. He hated to be wrong, but I couldn't help grinning.

'Tell you what Edward,' I said. 'Each morning you study the weather forecast in the newspaper and I'll use the weather house. We'll forecast the weather. Every time I get it right I can borrow your ball for the rest of that day. But if I get it wrong twice in a row you can have that voucher.'

Edward nodded, looking smug and sure of himself. We shook on it.

I was well pleased. After all, a weather house that is always wrong is as good as one that is always right! Unlike my clever clogs brother, Rain Boy knew that too. Out of the corner of my eye, I saw him wink at me.

Talking About the Story

Ask the Children

- Why did Joe want to practise his football every day?
- Why did he need another football?
- Why did Edward think he would win the bet?
- How did Joe know that he would win?

Points for Discussion

- The difference between truth and fact in real life and pretend in fiction. (Rain Boy could not wink in real life but we accept that it is true in the story. We call this a *suspension of disbelief*.)
- The difference between truth and lies in real life
- That if someone or something was always wrong we could know from this what was actually right!
- The difference between guessing something will happen and knowing it will happen. (*Knowing* often involves understanding cause and effect.)
- Have the children watched detective stories on TV? Discuss what kinds of things make good evidence for the police – forensic evidence is the strongest; witnesses may be more or less reliable. What kinds of things might affect witnesses?

Cross-curricular Story Activities

Key Stage 1 Activity

The children could paint a picture in which the weather is important: perhaps a storm at sea, a drought, a tsunami, fun or fear in the snow, lost in the fog, a sunny picnic leading to an adventure, etc.

Key Stage 2 Activities

1. Give the children copies of the photograph *Brown Bear in Snow* on page 47 (*Photocopiable Resource 8*). Write TRUE STATEMENTS on the board, and ask the children to make up some true sentences about the picture. For example,

the bear is brown. Snow is cold. When you have filled the blackboard with their correct suggestions, start again with FALSE STATEMENTS. Ask the children to make up some false sentences about the picture. For example, the bear is pink. There are leaves on the trees in the picture.

2. The children could watch a weather forecast on the television and, working individually or in pairs, write notes for their own pretend one. Some of these forecasts could be delivered to the class. What kind of weather are we expecting tomorrow – in Scotland, in Wales, in Ireland, in the different parts of England? And what about the rest of the week and the weekend?

Critical Thinking Activities

Key Stage 1 Activities

KS1 Activity 1: Logic and Sequence

Young children need to understand sequence as a preliminary to following logical argument.

Using story: very young children could draw scenes from stories in the correct order, e.g. Jack plants beans before a beanstalk can grow.

KS1 Activity 2: Cause and Effect

The children think about what must come first in relation to cause and effect. For example:

Hearing a joke and laughing

Heating metal and it expanding

Throwing up a ball before it falls down

Brainstorm other examples all round the class.

Key Stage 2 Activities

KS2 Activity 1: Rational Statements

Discuss with the children: which of the following statements are rational? Why/why not?

- I bet it will snow because I want to go on my new sledge.
- I think we should not go on the long drive because the forecast is for freezing conditions on the road.
- I think the other school will win the match because they have red shirts like Manchester United.
- I will take this medicine because the doctor said it will help to make me better.

NB: Construct some statements of your own to add to these.

Can the children themselves make up some rational and some irrational ones?

Ask the children to state something they believe in (e.g. honesty is a good thing; God exists; my pencil case is red; Ryan is a good swimmer) and they should justify their belief. The class discuss the justification. Was it convincing? Was it a good justification? Why/why not?

KS2 Activity 2: A Formal Debate

Debate is a good way for children to enjoy sharpening their ability to create good arguments and to criticize the reasoning of others. A formal debate is a form of public argument within a structured framework of agreed rules. A teacher can adopt a timeframe, rules and topic to suit the age, ability, size and interests of her class. At the most simple level, the teacher can be chair and have just one proposer and one opposer, with raised hands for general points made in support for one or the other side. After an agreed length of time, the debate will end with a vote.

KS2 Activity 3: Falsification

Give the children a copy of the photograph of the swan on page 50 (*Photocopiable Resource 9*). Explain to the children that at one time in England we believed that all swans were white. Only when a black swan was discovered in Australia was it recognized that not all swans are white. Philosophers and logicians used the sentence: 'All swans are white' to show that we only need one contrary instance to prove that the claim is wrong.

Let the children complete the exercise at the bottom of the picture.

For Enthusiastic and Gifted Children

1. At a more complex level of debate, two proposers and two opposers with two or more speakers to support or oppose the motion can be designated in advance. For large groups there can be two or more designated teams to propose and oppose.
2. Formal logic uses symbols in order to display the logical form of argument.

   If A happens then B will happen.
   A happens therefore B happens.

Some children will grasp simple logical structures and could be introduced to some formal logic.

Photocopiable Resource 8

Brown Bear in Snow

Interdisciplinary Project on the Weather

Many schools do topic work on the weather and these could be revisited and added to, incorporating some new ideas as follows:

English/Literacy

There are many weather-related poems in anthologies commonly used in schools. Read some of these with the children. After that the children can write their own poem which could be entitled: 'The Rain', or 'The Savage Storm' or 'Sunshine', etc. Younger children could draw a weather picture.

Science and IT

Focus on finding out more about global warming. Planet Earth is getting warmer, and this is blamed largely on the activities of humans. Scientists believe that humans have caused the earth to warm much more rapidly than at any other period in history.

Maths

Measuring rainfall. The children will need a clear plastic glass at least 10 inches tall, and a ruler or tape measure. Place the glass outside away from overhanging trees or eaves and make sure it is secure (i.e. it will not blow away in the wind). Leave the glass in place for at least one week, and at the same time each day measure the rainfall and record the observations. Use charts and graphs to present the information.

Geography

Look at weather patterns in different parts of the world and their effects on the population. Using maps and perhaps Google Earth, study the different weather systems throughout the globe, for example, the effect that the Gulf Stream has on our own weather patterns here in the UK. Other weather systems cause tornadoes, cyclones and hurricanes. These can have a devastating effect on human populations by destroying whole towns.

History and IT

Find out more about the history of weather forecasting. The study of weather is called meteorology. For millennia predicting the weather was done very informally. Since the late 1800s, weather forecasting has become more scientific and based on barometric pressures, precipitation and temperature. Agriculture depends on good weather forecasting. The children could look at how weather forecasting was done before the weather started to be formally recorded.

Art

Illustrate your weather story and/or poem.

Design and Technology

For the children to design their own weather house.

They can use three sides of a small cardboard box and paint this as a house. They could draw and then cut out a cardboard Rain Boy and cardboard Sunshine Girl. These should be glued onto a long stiff piece of wood or cardboard or perhaps something like a lolly stick. The card or wood should be made to swivel on a special fastener.

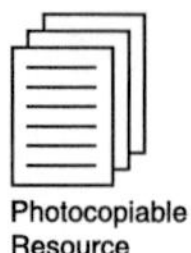

Photocopiable Resource 9

White Swan

All swans are white until you find a black one!

© Denise Taylor

Which of the following statements can be disproved? If they can be disproved, explain how.

- All trees drop their leaves in Autumn.
- It always rains in April.
- Mary is sad today.
- Dogs are better than cats.
- Fruit is good for you.
- Every cat has whiskers.
- All birds can fly.

CHAPTER

4 Tools of Critical Thinking: Finding Out

To ask questions is a way of finding out. To ask good questions is a way of deepening our own understanding, and at a more advanced research level may add to human knowledge. Young children can begin with simple fact-finding, which gradually develops into more extensive research projects.

Information can be acquired from a wide variety of sources including other people, books, the Internet and the mass media.

Explain to the Children

- Information can be acquired from other people, books, the Internet, newspapers and television.
- Think about the information given. Be critical! Ask questions! Consider whether it is well supported.

Skills

- The children need to learn how to find information and to find the best sources for the subject matter.
- They need to take a critical, questioning attitude and recognize when they should double-check.
- The children should become familiar with the school (and perhaps the local library) – learning how it classifies and stores its material.
- The children should learn how ICT and ICT skills can help with their finding out.

Preliminaries to the Story and Vocabulary

Research is searching carefully to find answers to questions, using a method to do this. Fynn and his classmates are searching for fossils. This will give them information and insight into what life was like on Earth millions of years ago, but they will need to uncover the fossils first of all, and then piece together all the information they can find.

The methods for research include planning and preparation, the research itself (the finding out) and, finally, reviewing and evaluating.

Vocabulary	
Fossil	the remains, impression or trace of a living thing that lived long ago in a different geologic age
Fascinated	to be enthralled; have one's interest or curiosity aroused by
Preserve	keep alive or in existence; make lasting
Scramble	climb or move quickly over rough ground using one's hands and feet
Disheartened	losing hope or courage; becoming dismayed
Inspecting	looking carefully at; viewing closely and critically
Landslide	a mass of soil or rock that is dislodged and falls down
Archaeologist	a person who studies history or prehistoric people by analysing their artefacts and other excavated remains
Partial	in part; not totally complete
Uncovered	having no cover or covering
Midsection	in the middle section or part of anything
Embedded	fixed into a surrounding mass
Irregular	without symmetry or even shape
Distinctive	having special quality, style, attractiveness; notable

A Piece of an Ancient Puzzle

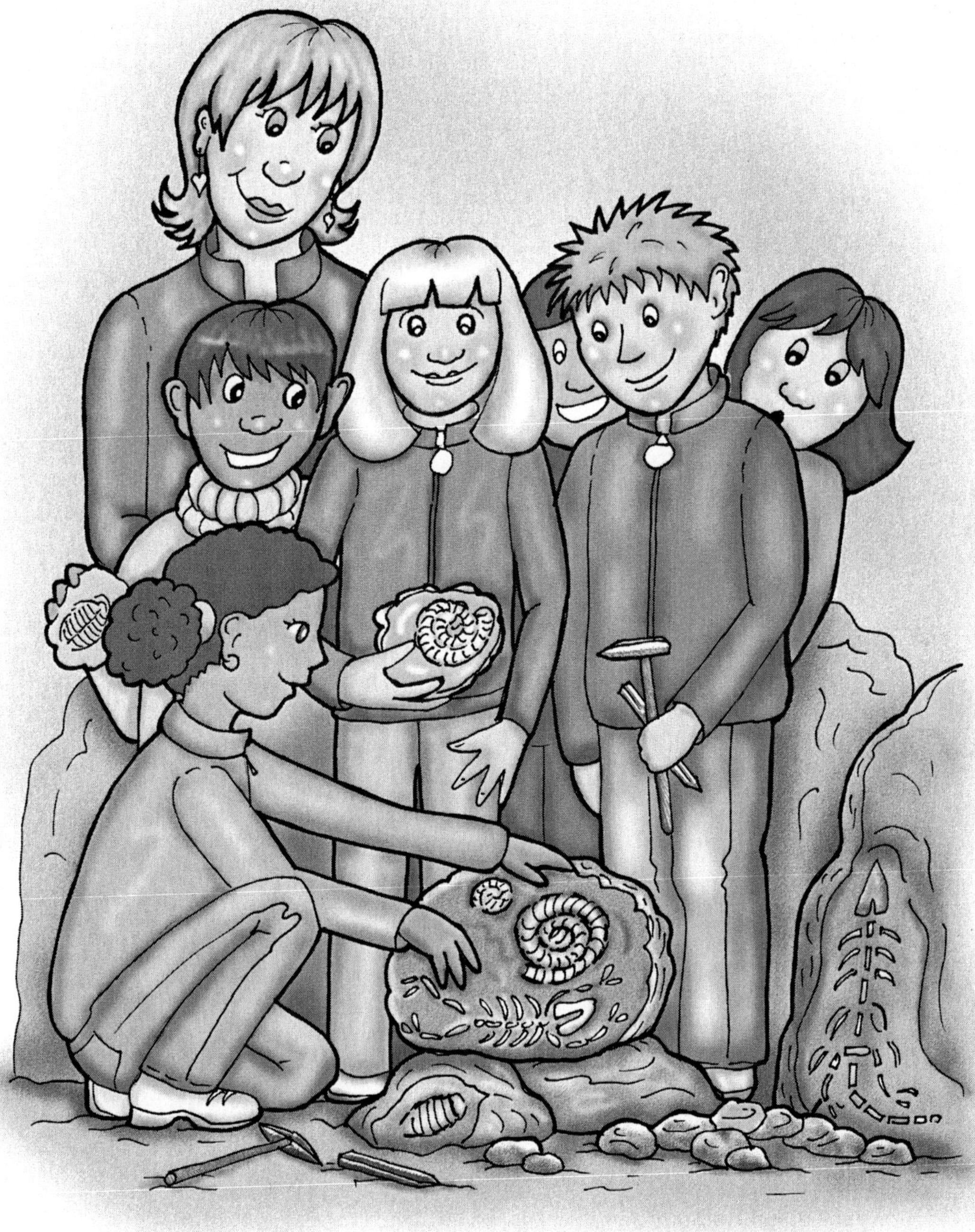

Photocopiable Resource

A Piece of an Ancient Puzzle

Fynn had spent the past hour and a half turning over stones and rocks, and had found nothing of any interest at all. He was really hoping to be the first one to find a fossil. Any fossil would do. His dad had told him so much about how the creatures that lived millions of years ago had been preserved in the rock, and that sometimes you can find the fossilized remains and see what the creatures might have looked like. He said fossils were like the pieces of an ancient puzzle, and sometimes you could solve the puzzle if you knew what you were looking for.

Fynn loved puzzles. As he dug, pulled and scraped at the rocks, he daydreamed about what life would have been like millions of years ago. There were no humans then. *That must have been really weird*, he thought. *A world without people.* He thought about what type of creature he would have been all that time ago. A dinosaur perhaps, or a sabre-toothed tiger or a dire wolf. Something big and scary. Definitely not something that would be eaten by bigger creatures.

'Hey Fynn, do you want to come and play in the rock pool with us?' asked Emily, suddenly appearing by his side, interrupting his daydreams about dinosaurs and tigers.

'No thanks,' said Fynn. 'I'm still hunting for fossils.'

'OK then. Good luck. Come and find us if you change your mind. See you later alligator,' she called over her shoulder, as she scrambled off over the rocks to play with the other children.

Fynn carried on turning over more rocks and stones, but still nothing. He was becoming very disheartened.

'Hi Fynn. Found anything yet?' Mr Shepherd, the class teacher, bent down next to him and started turning over rocks and stones, picking each one up and carefully inspecting it.

'Not yet. I've been looking for ages,' Fynn shrugged. 'There's nothing here.'

'Well. Maybe we're looking in the wrong place. Let's go and try over by the edge of the cliff. We found some really interesting

fossils there on last year's school trip. You'll have to be very careful though; the rocks are still loose after a landslide,' he warned. 'Come on, I'll show you the best place to look.'

The rocks by the cliff were different. They were bigger and more earthy than the other rocks he'd been looking at, which had been washed clean and smooth by the salty sea water. He took out his fossil-hunting hammer that his dad had bought him last Christmas. Somehow his search here felt more promising; more serious. He felt like a proper archaeologist.

A larger slab of rock caught his eye. It jutted out at a funny angle. Fynn struggled to turn it over by himself. It took all his strength, but eventually the rock moved and toppled over. He suddenly got butterflies in his tummy. Embedded in the rock was the outline of a skull and what looked like an arm or a wing.

'Sir, sir. Quick. Over here. I've found something,' Fynn shouted excitedly.

When the rock had been carefully cleaned, the children could all clearly see the partial outline of a creature that was the size of a small dog. The fossil Fynn had uncovered showed its head, and one foreleg. The rock had broken at the midsection of the fossil, which meant there was only the top half of the creature visible.

'We need to see if we can find the rest of the fossil,' said Mr Shepherd. 'Fynn, as you persevered with the fossil hunting when everyone else was bored with it, you should be the one to lead the rest of the class.'

Fynn's heart swelled with pride. He knew he would find a fossil today, and he had. Everyone walked to the spot where Fynn had been digging. They searched all afternoon, turning over more rocks and carefully scraping the earth away from the cliff face where the fossil had been found.

'It's like a jigsaw,' explained Mr Shepherd. 'We need to try and identify exactly where the piece of rock fell from.'

The children all studied the fossil. It had an irregular shape, and a distinctive pattern. They tried to match what they could

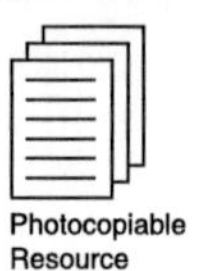
Photocopiable Resource

see on the fossil with the holes and spaces that had been left in the cliff face where the earth and rocks had fallen away. But too much earth had given way in the landslide and clambering over all the rocks and loose soil and sand made it really difficult.

Soon it was time to go. All the children got back on the coach and Fynn found himself the centre of attention. Everyone wanted to see the strange fossilized creature he'd found. He touched the large rock, which was now on the seat beside him. He couldn't wait to tell his dad. He would be so proud.

Talking About the Story

Ask the Children

- What is Fynn looking for on the beach?
- What tools does he use?
- What does he eventually find?
- Why do you think he had more success finding a fossil near the landslide?

Points for Discussion

- Information can be obtained from a variety of sources such as first-hand observation, books, journals and magazines, the Internet, other people, experts, photographs, films, artefacts.
- Effective research requires good primary and secondary questions, good planning, and sufficient resources to obtain the information being sought.
- The different methods of research and their alternatives need to be considered.
- Consideration also needs to be given to how the data will be analysed once it has been obtained.
- Asking questions is key to good research and curiosity should be encouraged.
- Some research projects require a good deal of perseverance. Fynn was tempted to go and play with the other children but his curiosity about life that existed millions of years ago motivated him to continue with his search. He was rewarded by finding a really good fossil. Discuss how perseverance and patience often brings rewards.

Cross-curricular Story Activities

Children are fascinated by fossils. They are a direct link to a past world that captures their imagination. They are also an ideal subject for inspiring creative work, developing critical thinking and providing a foundation for practising research skills.

Obtain an assortment of fossils and let the children handle and study them closely.

Key Stage1 Activities

1. Ask the children to sort the fossils into different groups by colour, and type of fossil (i.e. whether it is plant or animal).

2. Create a class collage with large sheets of paper depicting either a scene on land (perhaps in a forest) or an underwater scene (perhaps under an ocean). Using different brightly coloured materials such as paper, tin foil, wool, ribbon, different textiles, ask the children to create a small creature of their own to place on the collage.

Key Stage 2 Activities

1. Ask the children to study the fossils carefully. If the fossils are clear enough, the children could research the creature(s) that has been fossilized. What creature is it? What geological period is it from? What was the landscape like during that period (i.e. some landscapes were under the sea)? What other creatures lived at that time?
2. Use the Research Project Sheet on page 63 (*Photocopiable Resource 11*) to help the children with their research.

Critical Thinking Activities

The Research Process

There are a number of different stages to research. Depending on the complexity of the subject, the research activities could be carried out over a number of lessons, and on an interdisciplinary basis.

Getting Ready / Preparing

Discuss the different sources of information with the children and the different types of research methods. For younger KS1 children, it may be sufficient to explain the research methods in basic terms. For example, what they can do to 'find out' about things. KS2 children will require more in-depth explanation (for example, the different kinds of research – primary and secondary research; exploratory, constructive, empirical research; and qualitative and quantitative research).

Defining the Research Questions

Discuss some possible research questions. There are some examples below which relate to the story, but the children may also have subjects that they are particularly interested in that they wish to find out more about.

- How are fossils formed?
- When did dinosaurs live?
- What is sand?
- How old is the Earth?

Encourage the children to think about their own research questions for topics they are particularly interested in, perhaps a hobby or a subject they would like to know more about.

Carrying out the Research

Spend time explaining to the children how to obtain information. For example, use keywords to search the Internet and indexes in books, conducting experiments. Refer back to defining the research questions and some of the words used during that stage of the process.

Recording Information

Discuss the different ways of recording information. For simple research projects, it will be enough to write the answers down on the Research Project Sheet provided on page 63 (*Photocopiable Resource 11*). For more complex research subjects, older children could record their information in a variety of ways, and may also keep a journal of the research work to further encourage critical reflection. The children could also draw pictures and diagrams or take photographs or video recordings.

Analysing Data

For more complex research projects the data may need to be sorted and grouped into categories to identify patterns or trends.

Presenting the Findings

Depending on the complexity of the research project, allow the children time to present their findings. This could be done as a short presentation during Show and Tell or Circle Time, or it could be a whole class exhibition where all research projects are displayed in a poster format.

Making Crystals

Simple experiments are an ideal way for younger children to start learning about the different stages of the research process. Below is an experiment which makes crystals using vinegar and eggshells. The children can then follow the stages of the research process to record and present their findings. This experiment is easy to set up and monitor, and is safe for the children to handle.

Materials

- Approximately 250 ml **pickling vinegar** (or extra strength 7 per cent acetic acid by volume). Pure white vinegar (5 per cent acetic acid by volume) works as well but more volume needs to be used and less material may end up being dissolved.
- 3–4 crushed **eggshells**; the smaller the pieces the faster they will dissolve. (Alternatively, you can use small bits of gravel, limestone pebbles, chalk, marble chips or calcite.)
- **Containers** – 500 ml plastic tubs (yogurt, margarine, clear food containers). Clear containers make observation easier.

Method

- Pour vinegar into the small containers, and add the crushed egg shells, gravel or limestone.
- Observe the immediate reaction, and record this with a digital camera or make notes.
- Place the containers in a warm place where the ongoing reaction can be observed and recorded. The liquid will evaporate and deposition will occur, forming crystals.
- Check the containers regularly and record your observations. This can be done as a whole class with one journal for recording the changes, or in groups.
- After approximately three weeks, the liquid should have evaporated completely and crystals should have formed.

The children can use a variety of methods for recording their observations. They can keep a journal or diary of the changes they observe, they can draw pictures and diagrams, or they can take digital photographs.

Once the experiment has been completed, work with the children to analyse their findings.

The children can present their findings as a class display or exhibition, or as a presentation.

Discuss the whole research process with the children and the different stages of the experiment.

Finding out about Nature

Give the children a copy of the Research Project Sheet on page 63 (*Photocopiable Resource 11*), and a copy of the photograph on page 62 *Finding Out About Nature* (*Photocopiable Resource 10*). Use the subject in the photograph as an example to explain to the children the various stages of the research process. In the photograph, the children wanted to find out about frogs and lizards and their habitats (research question). They decided to carry out primary research by finding these creatures in the habitats in which they live. They observed the frogs and lizards first-hand, and then brought back some 'samples' to observe further. They documented their research by taking photographs, and drawing the different creatures (noting their size, colour and how they behaved).

Using this as an example, discuss with the whole class some possible research questions to choose from where they will need to use both primary and secondary research to find their answers. This could be on a current National Curriculum topic or theme, or they could conduct their own nature research or choose a topic of their own.

The children could use a mind-map or a spider-web diagram to outline the main areas of their research, with the primary question in the middle of the page, and secondary questions or topic headings in the branches or spokes of the diagram. Encourage the children to think of key words at this stage of the research, which will be useful later when carrying out Internet searches or using book indexes.

Allow sufficient time for the children to undertake their research, possibly over a period of a few weeks.

Discuss the various ways that the children can record their findings, and allow them to identify and choose the ones they prefer. (Later, discuss with the children whether their chosen research methods were the best ones to use.)

Once the children have completed their research project, allow time for them to present their findings. This could be in the form of a class exhibition or display, as a presentation to the class or school assembly, or in the form of a report or perhaps as a PowerPoint presentation, depending on the IT Suite resources.

Thinking Critically

Remind the children to:

- question the *relevance* of the information;
- question the *accuracy* of the information;
- question the *authority* of the information;
- question the *point of view* of the information;
- question the *fairness* of the information.

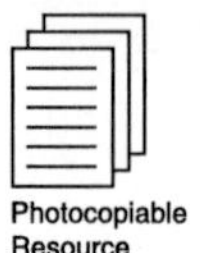

Photocopiable Resource 10

Finding Out About Nature

The two children in the photograph spent the day looking for lizards, frogs and toads. They observed the animals in their habitats, and learned first hand about where they lived and what they ate. The children created a mini habitat in a jar for a small green lizard, and studied it closely.

Photocopiable Resource 11

Research Project Sheet

Date	
Primary question	
Secondary or other questions	
Where can I look for the information?	
Who can I ask for information?	
Answer / Results	
Where I found my answer	
What I learned from the research	

Interdisciplinary Activities

Art

Fossils are imprints of living organisms that have become embedded in the surrounding environment. There are a number of art and creative activities that the children can do using the theme of fossils. For example: relief printing.

Relief Printing is printing from a raised surface, where a plate or stamp is made from materials such as wood, linoleum, metal, or even a potato. The children can draw a picture on the surface of the material and then, using different tools, cut away the areas that are not going to be printed – leaving the picture in relief. The children can experiment with different materials. Taking fossils as inspiration, the children can create pictures of imaginary creatures, or they could copy from real-life fossils.

Geography and History

Geology and geography are closely related subjects in that they both feature land-based topics that are linked to place. Fossil hunting uses knowledge of the types of rocks and materials that are the best for creating fossils, and where these can be located.

Activities around the fossil theme can include working with maps. For example, many of the fossils uncovered today are found in areas that were once covered by seas and oceans. The children will be surprised to find that there are sea shells and fossils of other marine creatures in areas where it would now be difficult to imagine that it was once a marine environment.

Studying rock formations and the fossilized evidence of life forms that were present on the earth millions of years ago can give children a sense of historical perspective. Using fossils and other historical artefacts from different ages and periods can be easily linked into themed topics in the curriculum. Learning about and imagining lives once lived is something children find fascinating, and this topic can be used to link to visits to museums or even to local quarries (if these are accessible in the local area).

CHAPTER

5 Tools of Critical Thinking: Analysis

Three key tools of analysis are: conceptual analysis, meta-analysis, and categorization and comparison.

Categorization and Comparison

Analysis involves recognizing or even creating categories. We break down our material in order to explore it. We classify material in order to gain a clearer overview. Comparisons (likening and contrasting) help such explorations.

Even young children can learn to categorize and to compare. They may, for example, put objects into groups according to their colour, or their function, or their shape. For example, they compare vehicles such as trains and cars, or apparently similar but very different things such as babies and dolls. To compare two objects the children think about ways in which they are alike, and ways in which they are different.

Conceptual Analysis

We can distinguish between concepts (ideas) and things – the idea of education (the meaning of the word in our minds) is not the same as the thing itself (the activities taking place in actual classrooms). To analyse the concept is to explore the use of the word in various contexts in order to get clearer about the ideas marked out by the word. This distinction is an unfamiliar one. It is perhaps easier for a child to understand the difference between a word and the thing itself.

Meta-analysis

'Meta' means 'above' or 'higher'. Meta-thinking is taking an overview (view from above) and also represents a higher (more critical) level of thinking skill. To be critical often requires that we move from ground level to meta-level thinking. The ground level is the information or the research findings, and the meta-level is the reflection on that ground-level information and research.

Explain to the Children

- When you look at two kinds of things (cars and trains) and think about how they are the same and how they are different, you will find you understand more about each of them. This is called making a comparison.
- The word 'table' is not a table – it is a word and you cannot eat off it! The thing table is not a word (the teacher points to a table and says 'it is this'). The word is not the same as the thing it names.
- We can also look at a piece of writing (a report, or a speech, or an argument), and we can ask questions about it. For example, do you agree or disagree? Why or why not? Do you believe it? Why or why not? Is it well supported with evidence? Is it wrong or right? Is it good or bad? This questioning is like looking down at the material to examine it. It is a bit like looking down from a high place as the boy does in the story (*The Disappearing Car*).

Skills

- The children should practise making comparisons to develop this skill.
- Ask the children to say things about a word (e.g. table has five letters), and to say things about the thing itself (e.g. some tables are writing tables and some are dining tables). Older children might see that the *idea* of table involves an object which supports different activities such as writing or eating.
- Encourage the children to take this critical overview of material to develop their ability to be analytic.

Preliminaries to the Story and Vocabulary

In this story the child hero wants to be a detective when he grows up. One day he has the chance to be a detective for real by looking down at the roads from the top of the cathedral tower, and watching where a stolen car is driven. He watches with patience. (Not easy when your nickname is Speedy because you tend to do everything in a rush!) Looking down and having an overview of the town below is symbolic of the meta-level tools of analysis practised in this chapter. The story might help the children to understand what you mean by 'looking over or down' at something. You might look down on (critique) a poem or a newspaper report or a picture or a story. Being a detective often requires looking at clues and working out a theory about what went on, just as being a scientist requires looking at phenomena (things that happen) and working out a theory to explain these. This connects with the importance of evidence, discussed in Chapter 3.

Vocabulary

Disappeared	vanished, went out of sight
Rush	hurry
Detective	a person whose job it is to investigate and find out
Patience	being able to wait and willing to take time and not to rush things
Roundabout	a circle of ground around which a car must drive
Robbers	thieves
Cathedral	large special church
Doubtful	unsure
Narrow	opposite of wide
Stolen	something taken by a thief
Worried	anxious
Swop	exchange
Glance	quick look
Cul-de-sac	a closed-in street like an avenue
Suspicious	looking as though he was up to no good
Search warrant	a certificate allowing the police to search a house or other building

The Disappearing Car

The Disappearing Car

'Speedy, don't gobble,' said Mum. Quickly Speedy scraped up the rest of his cereal into one mountainous spoonful and gulped it down before rushing outside to climb into the back of their new Alfa Romeo. *It's a cool car,* he thought. He liked it even more than the police car which his Dad, who was a policeman, sometimes drove home in.

'Seatbelt on,' said Dad, who was already in the driver's seat. Mum took the front passenger seat and the car's engine purred into action – a gentle but powerful sound.

'When I'm an adult,' Speedy said, 'I'm going to be a detective and catch robbers and have a car just like this one.'

They sped quickly to the cathedral and found an empty car space right by the car park entrance. Dad had to meet someone in the cathedral office and Mum wanted to look at the cathedral's stained glass windows. Speedy had just come along for the ride.

'Now don't rush round, son,' said Dad. 'Take your time. You'll never be a detective if you don't learn to have a bit of patience. You'll miss all the clues.'

Speedy, who longed to be a detective, decided there and then that he would stop rushing at things.

As he and Mum entered the cathedral, Speedy noticed the little ticket office for the tower.

'Wow, let's go up there Mum,' he pleaded, but Mum was looking doubtful.

'My ankle's not too good today,' she said.

'It's quite safe up there,' said the ticket lady. 'There's a great view and it's all glassed in.'

Mum's face cleared. 'Oh that's good! You can go up on your own,' she told Speedy, 'and I'll meet you back down here in half an hour. Hang on,' she added, as Speedy darted towards the tower's doorway. 'Let me get your ticket first!'

Speedy came back feeling foolish and mad at himself for rushing again. He took his ticket and was soon hurrying up the spiral staircase as fast as he could go.

Photocopiable Resource

The view from the top was amazing. Speedy moved all round looking down at the Legoland below him. He could see the roofs of small houses and tiny cars moving along narrow roads. He noticed the car park. He could see their new red Alfa parked right near the entrance where they had left it. But even as he looked down he was amazed to see the car reversing out of its parking space. Dad wouldn't leave without him. It was being stolen!

Speedy was just about to rush downstairs to tell Mum when he remembered Dad's words about patience and clues. He turned back. *I'll watch where it goes,* he thought. The car turned left out of the car park and first right onto a big housing estate. It curved around an island and went straight on before turning first left and then first left again. Speedy watched it as it moved alongside a house and disappeared into a garage. Now at last Speedy ran down the stairs as fast the wind and as speedy as his nickname. He ran his hand along the iron rail so that he wouldn't fall headlong down.

He found Mum and together they hurried to the office to tell Dad.

'Are you sure it was our car?' Dad said.

'Positive. I could see really clearly from the tower.'

'Let's go and take a look,' said the man who was with Dad. 'We can finish our discussion later.'

The four of them hurried to the car park. They stared at the empty space where Dad's car had been. Somehow even Speedy felt amazed to see that the car really had disappeared.

'I watched where it drove, Dad,' he said. He saw Dad and the other man exchange a glance.

'Worth a try,' the man said. 'Come on.'

They followed him to a dark blue car and climbed in. Speedy, feeling very important, was in the front.

'This is Stuart by the way,' Dad said to Mum and Speedy.

'Turn left out of the car park,' Speedy said. He was leaning forward, tense with excitement. 'Now take first right.'

The roundabout was nowhere in sight. Speedy felt anxious. Surely the car had curved round the island by now. His heart lurched when at last he saw it ahead. 'Yes!' he shouted. 'Straight on at the roundabout, then first left, and left again.'

They were soon in a big cul-de-sac.

'It's the house in the left hand corner,' Speedy said. The drive beside the house led to the blue doors of a double garage. 'It's in there.'

Speedy and Mum watched as Dad rang the doorbell of the house and spoke to the man who answered it. The man was shaking his head and soon closed the door. Back in the car Dad told them that the man had refused to open up his garage.

'Very suspicious, but we had no search warrant,' he added.

'He'll get rid of the car as soon as we've gone,' said Stuart.

'Get someone else to come and watch,' Speedy suggested.

'Just what I was thinking,' said Dad. He took out his mobile and phoned the local police station and suggested that an unmarked car should be parked on the road leading to the cul-de-sac. He gave the registration number of his stolen car and listened for a moment. 'Fine,' he said. 'Ten minutes then.' Dad looked at his watch and they waited. Speedy saw the man in the house look at them out of his window. The ten minutes seemed to pass very slowly indeed but at last they moved off.

A black car was parked in the road leading to the cul-de-sac and a woman with a shopping bag in her hand was nearby. As they passed she gave them a thumbs up sign and Dad drove past grinning.

'She'll jump in the car as soon as she sees my Alfa,' he told Speedy.

* * * * *

That evening Speedy heard a car turn into their drive. He peered out of the window and saw a black Honda, followed by Dad's new car.

'Dad,' he yelled, jumping up and down in excitement.

Photocopiable Resource

A policewoman and a policeman were soon drinking large mugs of tea with Speedy and Mum and Dad. Everyone was grinning broadly.

'The car thief drove to David Dean's used car place,' the policewoman explained. 'I followed and charged him. Even better, we've had our eye on Dodgy Dave's for some time. We suspected they dealt in stolen cars. This should nail them. All thanks to your quick thinking lad,' she added to Speedy. 'Not many kids would have stayed to watch exactly where the car went. They would have run straight down the tower to tell their Mum.'

'I nearly did,' said Speedy.

'Yes, he's usually quick off the mark,' said Mum.

'Well not when it matters,' said the policewoman. 'We'll have you on the force when you leave school.'

Everyone laughed.

'Actually, he does want to join,' Dad told the policewoman. He ruffled Speedy's hair.

'You did well today son. You learned how to be a detective for real.'

Talking About the Story

Ask the Children

- Why is the boy's name 'Speedy'?
- Why does Speedy go to the cathedral?
- Why could he see all the roads where the car went?
- Why was the policewoman pleased with Speedy?

Points for Discussion

- Talk about nicknames (kind and affectionate ones; unkind ones are a form of bullying, etc.).
- Talk about patience. Why is it called a virtue? In what ways can it be useful?
- Talk about theft. Why is stealing wrong? (It is unkind to the owner. It is dishonest. You wouldn't like your things to be stolen. It is against the law, etc.)
- Have the children experienced looking down from a high place? Where was it? What did they see? Connect this with critical thinking (taking an overview).

Cross-curricular Story Activities

Key Stage 1 Activity

Puzzles and Clues

Let the children 'play' the feel game. Divide the children into small groups. Have several objects on a tray covered by a cloth. Can the children in the group detect what the objects are simply by touch? (Change the objects for each group.) While their group is not doing the 'touching', the children could have a *jigathon*. That is, they could try to complete jigsaws of increasing difficulty. (We have to follow clues of colour and shape to complete a puzzle successfully.)

Key Stage 2 Activities

1. The children could write their own detective stories.
2. Let the children choose a detective novel to read. Later they could write reviews of the novel, including how the problem was solved, and giving reasons why they liked or did not like the story.

For Enthusiastic and Gifted Children

Encourage the children to think about clues and evidence and to build this into the detection in their story.

Critical Thinking Activities

Key Stage 1 Activities

KS1 Activity 1: Categorization – Compare and Contrast

1. Assemble and show a number of objects which the children will sort into meaningful categories (alternatively you could ask them to think about all the objects they can see in the classroom around them). Discuss the categories they could use. For example: group by colour or by shape or by size or by function, etc.

   NB: Objects that do not fit easily into the categories could be labelled **oddments** or **miscellaneous**. The children could work in groups, pairs or on their own.

2. Give each child a copy of the Photocopiable Resource on page 78. With this in front of them ask the children:

   - In what ways are the dog and the boy like each other? (For example: two eyes, one nose, one mouth, they live in houses, etc.)
   - In what ways are the dog and boy unlike each other? (For example: fur/skin/whiskers/no whiskers, etc.)
   - In what ways are the wolf and boy like each other? (For example: both have teeth, two ears, etc.)
   - In what ways are the wolf and boy unlike each other? (For example: four legs, two legs, they live in the wild or in houses etc.)
   - In what ways are the dog and wolf alike? (For example: both have fur and tails.)
   - In what ways are the dog and wolf unlike each other? (For example: dogs live with people, they are domesticated. Wolves live in their own family groups in the wild.)

Now ask the children to complete the sentences on their sheet (*Photocopiable Resource 12*). You could write words the children will need onto the board.

3. **Kinds of Things**

Give each child a copy of the photograph *Cityscape*, on page 79 (*Photocopiable Resource 13*). Ask the children to:

- Find two different kinds of vehicle.
- What are the vehicles (e.g. boat, car, train)?
- Find as many different objects as they can. What are they?
- List how many different kinds of objects they can see. What are they? (e.g. sky/water/brick; floating objects/moving objects/stationary objects, tall objects/low objects, etc.)

The children could try to draw their own 'looking down' picture.

Ask the children:

- Do you like this photograph? Why/why not?
- In what ways (or situations) can an overview photograph help us?

KS1 Activity 2: Analysis

Read something to the children which you know they will find of interest. Ask the children to say in their own words what the piece was about. Now ask the following questions:

- Did you like the piece? Why/why not?
- What might make the piece even more interesting?
- Can you add your own ideas/experiences about this subject?

Key Stage 2 Activities

KS2 Activity 1: Categorization – Compare and Contrast

Have the children complete the sentences on page 78 (Photocopiable Resource 12 as for KS1 above). Additionally, the children then write a short piece, comparing dogs with wolves, or dogs with people.

KS2 Activity 2: Conceptual Analysis

Choose a fairly complex abstract idea which will be of interest to the children and which relates to their experience in some way. Have a discussion about this.

To encourage conceptual analysis (thinking about the meaning of abstract words or ideas) say 'good point' whenever they make a conceptual point i.e. a point about the concept, not the thing. E.g. Education is boring (the thing), education helps you understand (good point). You learn about democracy in politics (the thing). Democracy means everyone has a fair vote (good point). I don't like homework (the thing). Homework is the work given at school to do at home (good point). I got loads of presents for Christmas (the thing). Christmas is a Christian celebration (good point).

KS2 Activity 3: Meta-analysis

Select a piece of prose that is making a case or making an argument that would interest your pupils and be appropriate to their age and ability. Read and discuss this piece with the class and then simply ask them to answer the questions.

Say/write in your own words what this piece is saying.

- Do you like this piece? Why/why not?
- Do you agree with it? Why/why not?
- Can you think of any other point to support the piece?
- Can you think of a point that would be against the piece?
- What would make this piece work better? (For example, what would make it easier to understand or more interesting?)

KS2 Activity 4: Media Studies

Encourage the children to take a critical stance to advertisements. Explain that advertisers are trying to **persuade** you to buy their product and may exaggerate how good it is and make misleading claims about it. They will make the packaging look attractive with striking colours and patterns and lively, catchy (easy to remember) slogans and names.

Collect as many colourful adverts from magazines as you can. Free supermarket magazines may be useful and you could ask the children to bring some in too.

The children work in small groups. Give each group five or six of the cut out advertisements. They should analyse each one. Give each group a copy of The Media Studies Prompt Sheet (*Photocopiable Resource 14*) on page 80 to help them.

NB: Subsequently the children might enjoy designing their own persuasive advertisements – practising artwork, design, and good use of words!

For Enthusiastic or Gifted Children

Conceptual Analysis

Take two linked ideas and see how many overlaps or differences they can find. For example, education/indoctrination; writing story/telling a story; swimming/floating; democracy/dictatorship.

Photocopiable Resource 12

Compare and Contrast

Dog	Boy	Wolf

© Denise Taylor

1. The boy and the dog both. . . . .

2. Only the boy. Only the dog. . . . .

3. The boy and the wolf both . . . .

4. Only the boy. . . . . Only the wolf . . . .

5. The dog and the wolf both . . . .

6. Only the dog . . . . Only the wolf . . . .

Photocopiable Resource 13

Cityscape

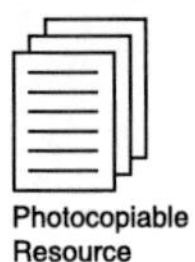

Photocopiable Resource 14

Media Studies Prompt Sheet. For Advertisement Analysis

- Is the advertisement clear?
- Do you agree/disagree with what is being claimed? Why?
- Are any arguments or evidence presented?
- Are they sound?
- Is the advertisement fair, honest, misleading, biased?
- Are there assumptions being made?
- Do you agree with these?
- Who is the advertisement aimed at, i.e. what kinds of people: young or old, male or female, rich or poor etc?
- Is the advertisement attractive to look at?
- Is the name of the product (or the slogan used) a good one? Why/why not?
- Would you buy this product? Why/why not?
- Do you know of alternative products? Are these better/worse?
- To sum up, in your opinion, is this a good (persuasive) advertisement or a poor one?

PART 2
Philosophical and Moral Reflection

CHAPTER

6 An Introduction to Philosophy

Children are naturally full of wonder at the existence of things and often ask deep (philosophical) questions – that is questions that cannot be answered scientifically. They cannot be answered by the scientific methods of observation and experiment, and therefore can only be answered through reflection.

Philosophers are concerned with meaning and with truth/knowledge. They ask: 'What do we mean by …?', and 'How do we know that …?' Because philosophers work by thinking about concepts/ideas/meanings rather than by conducting experiments as the scientists do, introducing children to philosophy encourages them to be more reflective and analytic. It also taps into their sense of wonder and connects with deeper topics which they find of interest.

To engage in philosophical reflection is to practise critical thinking on philosophical questions. Such questions arise in different areas such as ontology (concerned with what there is), epistemology (theory of knowledge) and ethics (theory of value and the nature of morality).

One important distinction is that between *substantive* and *analytic* philosophy. Substantive philosophy seeks to construct a system of belief about the 'good life' and the 'good society'. The philosopher is trying to work out an actual answer about how we should live. Analytic philosophy, on the other hand, seeks to use the critical tools of philosophy (conceptual analysis and meta-reflection) about non-empirical questions. The philosopher is not expecting to find a concrete answer so much as to gain greater understanding.

Explain to the Children

- Philosophy is about questions which cannot be answered by experiments, but only through reflection. There are no right or wrong answers – only ideas and insights which deepen our understanding.
- By thinking about such questions we become more clear about fundamental, important questions about ideas, knowledge, existence, goodness and so on.
- In substantive philosophy there are many different philosophies, that is, systems of belief about how we should live our lives. In analytic philosophy there are different approaches to reflection and analysis.

Skills

The children will develop philosophical skills and understanding by engaging with philosophical questions. Practice in **doing** philosophy brings the skills and understanding.

Preliminaries to the Story and Vocabulary

Fishing for Stones links with philosophy in a number of ways:

- The beauty and variety of stones is a source of wonder at what there is – an ontological wonder (the awe that they exist!). This wonder leads us to ask why there are stones and clouds, sky and water, people and fish and sunshine and light. Why does this wonderful universe exist? What kinds of things exist?
- Philosophers often talk of a 'category mistake' where confusion arises from ascribing an object to a wrong category. 'Fishing for Stones' sounds like a category mistake.
- Stones are a kind of symbol for what seems to be the brute fact of the existence of the external world. They have an existential quality that seems undeniable in the face of sceptical doubts and of the problem of perception covered in Chapter 10.

Vocabulary	
Wonderful	amazing
Gaze	look hard at
Attached	joined
Bamboo cane	a long stick made of bamboo wood
Jammed together	crammed in
Disappointed	felt let down
Grumpy	bad tempered
Exchanged	swopped
Peaceful	quiet and gentle
Dancing patterns	the light moved making different shapes
Enchanted	magical
Intent	focused on
Speckled	dotted with marks
Collected	gathered together
Marvelled at	wondered at
Presented	gave

Fishing for Stones

Photocopiable Resource

Fishing for Stones

'Look Iris,' said Rosie, pointing at the orange fishing nets. Her voice was shiny with excitement. 'Let's buy one each.'

Iris and Rosie had recently moved to a new house with a stream nearby.

'What about Mum's birthday?' said Iris. 'We saved up to buy her a present, remember. We didn't come shopping to buy something else instead!'

'But Iris, Dad will put our names on his present. Anyway, it's not 'till Wednesday. We could make something by Wednesday. She said she likes homemade things the best.'

'I don't think she does really.'

'Oh come on Iris! Think how wonderful it will be to catch some fish. I really, really, really want to.'

Iris gazed at the fishing nets. They were in the centre of the shop window – each net attached to a bamboo cane and all jammed together into a long vase like huge orange flowers.

Iris imagined dipping one into the stream and pulling out a big silver fish. She forgot about Mum's birthday.

'OK,' she said.

The girls bought their nets and hurried to the stream and dipped them into the flowing water. They lifted them eagerly at first to peer in as the water drained away. They became increasingly disappointed. They fished for about an hour and not a single fish was caught.

'We might as well give up,' Iris said. 'I wish we had bought Mum's present now!'

'I've got one,' Rosie yelled, making Iris jump.

She watched Rosie lift a heavy dripping net. In it rested a large, round stone. Rosie glared at it. The stone was a dark red colour with a clear white marble line down the middle. Iris could tell that Rosie was very disappointed.

'What a beautiful stone Rosie,' Iris said. 'Tell you what, why don't we fish for beautiful stones? Only lovely ones mind. Ones

that will look nice on Mum's stony flower bed. Mum said it really needs some more stones.'

'Why?' said Rosie. She sounded grumpy.

'The plants there need a stony ground to grow in. Mum told me. You know how she loves her plants. The stones could be her birthday present!'

Rosie's frown was exchanged for a smile.

Iris enjoyed fishing for the stones. After living in a busy town she loved the peaceful countryside. Above her head white clouds made slowly changing patterns on the deep blue sky while at her feet sunshine made dancing patterns of light on the gently flowing stream.

'It's like being in an enchanted garden in a storybook,' she said to Rosie, but Rosie was too intent upon her task to answer her.

Any stones which the girls didn't like were thrown back into the stream, making a lovely plop. The stones they did like were added to a small, growing hill of good finds. Green stones, dark red stones, speckled stones, stones shaped like frogs and lonely stones that seemed to want to be collected. Iris marvelled at all the different kinds of stones to be found in one small stream. She felt happy to have such a lovely gift for Mum's birthday.

On the way home Iris' and Rosie's nets were full of heavy stones. Rosie carried her net over her shoulder. Iris cupped her hands under the orange netting of hers. It was hard work carrying their nets but they struggled back to their garden where they hid the stones under a hedge.

'Oh no,' said Rosie, 'my net is torn. It's no good for fishing now.'

'Never mind Rosie,' said Iris. 'There are no fish in that stream anyway, and we can pick out stones with our hands whenever Mum needs any more.'

'For her next birthday,' Rosie suggested.

'No, Rosie. We're definitely buying a present for that one!'

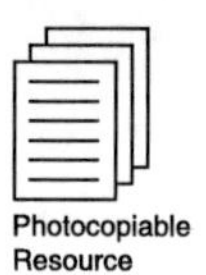

Two days later, on Mum's birthday, Iris and Rosie presented her with the beautiful stones. Mum examined every one, exclaiming over their colours and patterns. Carefully she took them and placed them in the stony pathway, dotting them about to look pretty. She was very pleased.

Talking About the Story

Ask the Children

- Why had Rosie and Iris saved up their money? What did they buy instead?
- How did Iris feel about this later?
- What different kinds of stones did they find?
- What did the girls give their Mum for her birthday?

Points for Discussion

(there are no wrong answers)

- Iris felt guilty about spending the birthday present money. Have a discussion about guilt. (Moral reflection is one kind of philosophical reflection and will connect with the next chapter. When do we feel guilty? Is guilt a good or a bad thing? How do we know we have done a wrong thing? Have you ever felt guilty? What did you do about it? What could you have done?
- Iris felt awed by the variety of beautiful stones. What other things in nature are wonderful? (Examples are flowers, waterfalls, mountains, seahorses etc.)
- Why does this wonderful world exist?
- What different kinds of things exist in the story (people, water, clouds, stone etc.).
- What categories could we put these each into (for example solid/not solid; living/inanimate; natural/man-made; moving/stationary)?
- By the end of the story do the girls know that there are no fish in the stream?
- Do they know that there are stones in the stream?

Cross-Curricular Story Activities

Key Stage 1 Activity

The children could draw a picture of something in nature that they find wonderful or they could do their own illustration of *Fishing for Stones*.

Key Stage 2 Activity

The children could write a poem called *This Wonderful World*.

For Enthusiastic or Gifted Children

You could read the poems *Glory be to God for Dappled Things* (Gerard Manley Hopkins) and *The Great Lover (These I have Loved)* (Rupert Brooke). The children could write (poem or prose) about the things which they like.

Philosophical Thinking Activities

Key Stage 1 Activities

KS1 Activity 1: Questions, Learning and Reflection

Choose some interesting objects and ask the children to think up some questions about each one. (For example, a conch shell. What is it? Where was it found? Can you hear the sea when you put it against your ear? A model dinosaur. What is it? What kind of dinosaur is it? Are there dinosaurs alive now?) The children will experience how much they can learn about something by asking questions. Encourage them to develop their own points of view about non-empirical questions by encouraging discussion (for example, why are shells beautiful? Why do we like dinosaurs?)

KS1 Activity 2: Questions and Answers

Give the children copies of the complex tree photograph on page 92 (*Photocopiable Resource 15*). The children copy down the following words: tree, light, colour, sun, leaves, grass, green. Can they write a question and its answer on the next page? For example, what is making the light? The sun is making the light. What colour is the grass? The grass is green. What is in the picture? A tree is in the picture. Now encourage the children to experience the wonder captured by this photograph – the wonder of the sun, stars and planets; the wonder of living things (trees, leaves, people and animals); the wonder of light and all the beautiful things that light enables us to see.

Key Stage 2 Activities

KS2 Activity 1: Empirical and Philosophical Questions. Which are Which?

Which of the following questions are scientific? (You find the answer by observing the world or doing an experiment. You discover facts.) Which questions are philosophical? (You cannot answer them by finding facts. You try to answer them by thinking about them!)

1. Should you feel guilty if you bully someone?
2. Will I be punished if the teacher catches me bullying someone?
3. Does the sky really exist like stones do?
4. Can I know there are no fish in the stream?
5. How many clouds are in the sky today?
6. Does God exist?
7. Did God create the universe?
8. How can I know that you feel pain like I feel pain?

Working in pairs the children could make up some scientific (factual) questions of their own. They could make up some philosophical (reflective and non-factual) questions too.

KS2 Activity 2: Writing Your Reflections

Let the children choose one of the philosophical questions above and write a short piece about what they believe and why.

For Enthusiastic or Gifted Children

The story photograph depicts sunlight through a tree. Both objects (light and trees) have a philosophical resonance. Let the children discuss the following philosophical question about trees:

> *If a tree falls in a forest and there is no one there to hear it fall, does it make a sound when it falls?*

Light – questions about light are at the cutting edge of theoretical physics and seem to merge with philosophy. For example, can light be both a wave **and** a particle? Some of the children could find it interesting to use the IT suite to find out more about what we know about light.

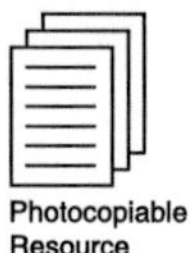

Photocopiable Resource 15

Sunlight through Tree

Questions and Answers

CHAPTER

7 Ethics and Morality

To think about right and wrong or moral goodness, and to try to work out how we should act in the right way, or to try to solve a moral dilemma, we need to reflect about it. Just as with philosophical questions, ethical ones are not answered scientifically, but by engaging in critical reflection. These reflections will be informed by principles of justice and by empathy and compassion towards others (and non-human creatures).

We explore ethical and moral problems using the thought patterns identified in Chapter 1, the concern for justification identified in Chapter 2, and the tools of analysis explored in Chapter 5. For example, conceptual analysis will focus on concepts such as right, good, moral, value, and so on.

Morality is concerned with character or conduct considered as good or evil, and ethics is the branch of philosophy with character and conduct.

The field of values is a complex one. We believe our moral judgements are in some sense objective, and yet we can have very different judgements because of value differences between us.

Explain to the Children

- Explore moral vocabulary with the children: good and bad, right and wrong, duty and obligation, moral responsibility, human rights, animal rights.
- Sometimes we are told: 'Do as you would be done by.' This is similar to what is called the principle of universalizability i.e. the idea that we should only engage in an action if the principle behind it is one that you would be happy if everyone adopted. For example: 'Never start a fight, but defend yourself if you are attacked' might be a moral principle which you would be happy to universalize. However, 'Murder people you don't like' would not be a moral principle as you would certainly not like someone to murder you.
- Moral reflection and moral actions pay attention to the well-being of others and being fair.

Skills

- To understand moral terms.
- To be able to distinguish between values and preferences.
- To be able to distinguish between facts and values.
- To be able to apply the aspects of critical thinking to moral dilemmas.
- To understand what it means to be fair and to act fairly.
- To develop empathy and compassion through personal, social and moral education.

Preliminaries to the Story and Vocabulary

The story is about the importance of friendships, establishing a basis of trust and about the promises we make to our friends. The children break their promise to their friends because they want to help them. In this situation, there is probably just cause to do this (this is known as conflict of values), but this raises the question of when it is right or wrong to break promises, what promises we can break and which ones we should keep or honour.

Children learn all the time about values, strength of character and moral conduct through interactions and experiences with their peers. They learn about keeping promises, lies and deception, and right and wrong behaviours. Caring behaviour includes helping friends and being compassionate. Bad behaviour includes bullying, telling malicious lies and being unkind to others.

Using moral dilemmas as examples in a school setting helps children to understand about values and what they should and shouldn't do in certain situations.

In this story, the children promise to keep a secret, but in the end they break their promise and tell their mother. As well as discussing the issues of moral dilemmas, the teacher could use this story to discuss when to keep secrets and confidences and when not to. It is important that children understand when they can break a confidence and tell an adult or carer about any concerns they might have.

Vocabulary	
Sprite	an elf, fairy or goblin
Snout	the nose of an animal
Unawares	without warning, by surprise, to be caught off-guard
Sprawling	stretched or spread out
Ancient	very old
Rotation	moving round
Synchronized	moving at the same time and exactly together
Boughs	branches of a tree, especially a larger one

Burst	break forth suddenly and forcibly
Startled	receive a sudden shock or alarm
Bole	the stem or trunk of a tree
Amazement	overwhelming surprise or astonishment
Scared	frightened
Imagination	forming mental images of what is not actually present
Approached	came near or nearer to
Ploughing	turning up soil with a plough, or make a furrow

A Spritely Promise

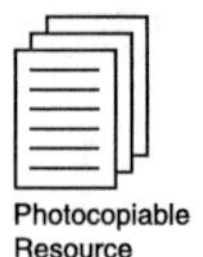
Photocopiable Resource

A Spritely Promise

Ellie and Luke first saw the forest sprites on a beautiful, hot day in the middle of summer. They were out walking with their dog, Brock, who looked like a badger, with a big white strip across his head and down his snout.

The sprites were busy chasing each other round and round a sprawling oak tree; an ancient tree that was the last surviving one in a big field now used to grow crops of maize, barley and wheat. This year it was maize, which was tall and strong as it swayed in the wind like long rows of synchronized dancers.

Brock disappeared into the maize following the scent of a fox, and Ellie and Luke dashed after him. He suddenly burst out of the maize, startling the playful sprites, who immediately ran for cover, and dived into a small hole in the bole of the tree. Ellie and Luke caught sight of them just as they disappeared.

'Wow,' gasped Ellie in amazement. 'Did you see that?' They had heard about sprites, fairies and goblins in fairy stories, but never thought they would ever see any.

The breeze had now become so strong that the mighty boughs of the tree creaked and groaned.

'The tree is singing,' said Ellie. 'Listen!' They both stopped and listened. The sound was both beautiful and eerie at the same time.

Luke bent down and called into the hole. 'We won't hurt you. We're really sorry we scared you. Please come out.' But there was no sign of the sprites. Ellie and Luke now began to wonder whether they had actually seen them or whether it was just a trick of the light or their imaginations running wild.

They spent most of the summer playing by the tree. They had picnics there, and would spend long afternoons reading books and magazines, and listening to the sound of the wind singing through the leaves and branches. They didn't see the sprites again and forgot all about them.

Then one day, when it was very windy, they arrived at the tree, and heard music and laughter just like the first time they

had seen the sprites. This time they approached the tree very cautiously and quietly. The sprites were jumping from bough to bough, and laughing as they tagged each other.

'Hello,' said Ellie in a gentle whisper. The sprites stopped their chasing, and stood on the lowest branch of the tree, looking down at them. 'We won't harm you,' said Ellie. 'We just want to be friends.'

Suddenly, the female sprite dropped to the ground, ran towards Ellie, tapped her on the arm, and said: 'Tag. You're it!' She scampered off around the tree.

Ellie squealed with delight, and ran after her, but the sprite was very quick and was soon swinging back up into the tree.

The long summer holidays passed slowly and the children and the sprites became the best of friends. They learned that the sprites were called Neboah and Filigrim, and that they lived in a big space underneath the tree.

As autumn approached the crops were harvested, and the tree stood out in the bare field. It was almost time to start back at school.

'We will really miss playing with you every day,' Ellie said sadly.

'Yes, but you will have all your friends at school to play with instead,' said Neboah. 'And you can still come to see us at the weekends.'

'Yeah, everyone is going to be amazed about our adventures with you. I can't wait to tell them,' said Luke excitedly.

A look of complete shock came over Filigrim's face. 'You must never ever, ever tell anyone about us,' she said sternly. 'You must promise.'

Ellie and Luke were disappointed that they couldn't share their news with their school friends, but they both said: 'We promise!'

'Why is it so important that we don't tell anyone though?' asked Luke.

'Our homes in the forest have already been destroyed. The last few trees here on this land are the only ones left. If people find

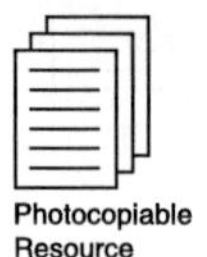

out about us, they will be curious about us, and we will never be safe.'

Although they were really disappointed, Ellie and Luke understood, and swore that they wouldn't tell anyone.

* * * * *

The children went back to school and faithfully kept their secret about their newfound friends, and didn't breathe a word to anyone. All winter they went to play with Neboah and Filigrim each weekend, and their friendship grew stronger and stronger.

One beautiful spring day they saw three men by the tree. They had clipboards and tape measures, and wore hard yellow hats and bright yellow coats over the top of their suits. They were measuring the tree and writing things down. Ellie and Luke returned home very worried. They had not seen anyone else by the tree before. What was happening? Why were they taking measurements? Was something going to happen to the tree?

'We have to find out what's going on,' declared Luke. 'Let's go and ask the farmer. He's bound to know what's happening.'

That afternoon, they saw the farmer on his tractor ploughing another field. They waved to him and he came over to speak to them.

'Hello,' he said. 'I saw you waving. Are you OK? Is there something wrong?'

'We saw some men by the oak tree in the big field. Is something going to happen to it? Only it's our favourite tree,' said Ellie.

'Oh dear!' said the farmer. 'I'm really sorry. That old tree has to come down for the new road that's being built. The men you saw were working out the best way to chop it down.'

'No!' cried Ellie. 'You can't chop it down. It's ....'

Luke tugged Ellie's sleeve sharply, and glared at her. 'Thanks for telling us,' he said to the farmer. 'Come on, Ellie. We've got

to get home now.' He dragged her away before she could say anything else.

When they were out of earshot of the farmer, he turned to her and said, 'You nearly gave the game away, silly. We promised we wouldn't tell anyone.'

Ellie and Luke spent the next few days desperately worried about what to do. They tried as hard as they could to think of a solution to help Neboah and Filigrim, but although they wracked their brains, there was nothing they could think of to stop their friends' home from being destroyed.

Their school friends all noticed their sad mood, and asked them what was wrong.

'Nothing!' Ellie and Luke replied. 'We're fine.' But it was obvious to everyone that they weren't.

'You've both been like this for days now,' their Mum said, worriedly. 'What on earth is the matter?'

'We can't tell you,' they said.

'Why ever not?'

'Because we made a promise!' explained Luke, looking even more downhearted than ever. If they couldn't even tell Mum, then who could they tell?

Their Mum smiled at them. 'You know, a problem shared is a problem halved,' she said, trying to cheer them up. 'And if you do tell me, I promise not to tell a soul about your promise. Cross my heart.'

'You're right,' Luke agreed. 'We should tell you. But you're never going to believe us.'

Ellie nodded. *Mum knew all about tree preservation orders,* she thought. *She just might be able to save the tree.*

Talking About the Story

Ask the Children

- Why did the sprites not notice Ellie and Luke at first?
- Why was the tree singing?
- What promise did Ellie and Luke make to the sprites?
- Where did the sprites live in the tree?
- Why was the tree going to be pulled down?
- What do you think would happen to Neboah and Filigrim if their home was destroyed?
- What does Ellie and Luke's Mum mean when she says 'A problem shared is a problem halved'?
- Were the children right to break their promise to their friends? Can you think of anything else they could have done?

Points for Discussion

- Explain to the children the importance of keeping promises that they make.
- Ask the children whether they think Ellie and Luke were right to break their promise to Neboah and Filigrim. Why/why not?
- In the story the promise is made to make-believe characters. Ask the children whether they think this makes the promise they make more important or less important? Why/why not?
- Discuss with the children when it is important to keep a secret or confidence and when it is important for them to tell an adult or carer if they have any concerns or problems they would like to discuss.
- The children could discuss different situations where environmental values clash with other social needs, as in the story with the old tree and the building of the new road.

Cross-curricular Story Activities

Select four or five well-known fairy tales that highlight good use of moral dilemma.

Key Stage 1 Activities

1. Ask the children to choose their favourite hero/heroine or villain and draw or paint a picture of them.
2. Use the children's pictures for a class discussion on right and wrong, and good and bad. For example: this is a picture of X from the story. Do you think he/she is good or bad? What do you think they did that was right/wrong?

Key Stage 2 Activities

1. Ask the children to choose which particular stories or themes they like the best from the fairy stories discussed, and to write their own story which contains a hero/heroine and a villain or villains.
2. After the children have completed their stories, select ones that show good or bad, and right or wrong, and discuss these with the children. Encourage the class to debate the moral issues in the stories.

For Enthusiastic or Gifted Children

The children could develop the theme further into a role play scenario or piece for drama.

They could also be asked to provide examples of moral dilemmas from watching television programmes or films or from reading newspapers and magazines. The children could then select a few examples to be used in further class debate or discussion.

Critical Thinking Activities

Classroom discussions and activities about values and moral dilemmas provide a safe environment for children to consider, sometimes for the first time, what they believe is right or wrong, good or bad, and why or why not. Some discussions may be informal and may arise as a result of an incident or situation that has occurred in school or in the classroom. Other activities can be more formally introduced to the children as exercises for them to complete.

During values discussions it is important to focus on the morality issues of what *should* be done and the justifications the children offer. Listening to, and reflecting on, the reasons given by their peers is also important.

Using moral dilemmas as part of classroom activities can take the form of a class debate, an open class discussion, or role play or drama. There are some examples of moral dilemmas on page 107 (*Photocopiable Resource 17*). Stories (especially fairy tales), films and television programmes can also provide a rich resource of moral dilemmas that can be used in critical thinking activities. Children may also want to discuss their own dilemmas that occur in their day-to-day lives.

Before undertaking more formal activities, teachers should familiarize themselves (and the children where appropriate) with the characteristics of discussions about moral dilemmas:

An open-ended approach: In many cases there is no single 'right answer'. The goal is not to reach agreement but to critically discuss the reasons used to justify a recommended action. The emphasis is on why some reasons may be more appropriate than others.

Free exchange of ideas: The children should feel comfortable in expressing their thoughts. They should have an opportunity to contribute to the discussion within a non-judgemental atmosphere.

Development of listening and verbal skills: Each student should be intimately engaged in the discussion activity, building and expanding on one another's ideas as well as examining each response critically.

Focus on reasoning: The emphasis should be on reasoning that highlights the prescriptive 'should' and 'ought' (the moral imperatives).

Dilemmas produce conflict: Moral dilemmas are about resolving internal conflict and reflecting on what course of action should be taken. Discussions about some dilemmas could also lead to conflict within the classroom, and it is important to reflect on the points above about an openness of expression, developing listening skills and reflecting upon another's point of view.

Adapted from '*Conducting Dilemma Discussions in the Classroom*', WWNFF Institute, July 1992

Key Stage 1 Activity

KS1 Activity 1: Moral Dilemmas

Children at KS1 tend to view moral dilemmas in a more absolute way, and readily accept the direction and instruction of adults or people in authority. They tend to accept the things they are told at face value and do not question the underlying assumptions.

When discussing moral dilemmas with children at this stage, use simple examples of right or wrong, good or bad.

Key Stage 2 Activity

KS2 Activity 1: Moral Dilemmas

By KS2, most children are starting to question assumptions. They generally have a sense of right or wrong, good or bad, and can make clearer distinctions. They will start to recognize that some moral dilemmas do not have one right or wrong answer, and that some answers may depend on social and cultural influences.

An interesting ethical discussion to have with KS2 children is one based on altruism and altruistic species.

Altruism is defined as an action that benefits the receiver but comes at a cost to the giver or performer. Someone who is said to be altruistic will often put others before him or herself.

Hold a values and ethics discussion with the class and discuss examples of altruism. Ask the children to think of cases where they would help others, and 'do the right thing', and cases where they would not. Discuss the reasons for their answers, and within the framework of conducting moral discussions, open up the debate within the class setting so that different opinions are shared constructively.

Photocopiable Resource 16

The Mighty Tree

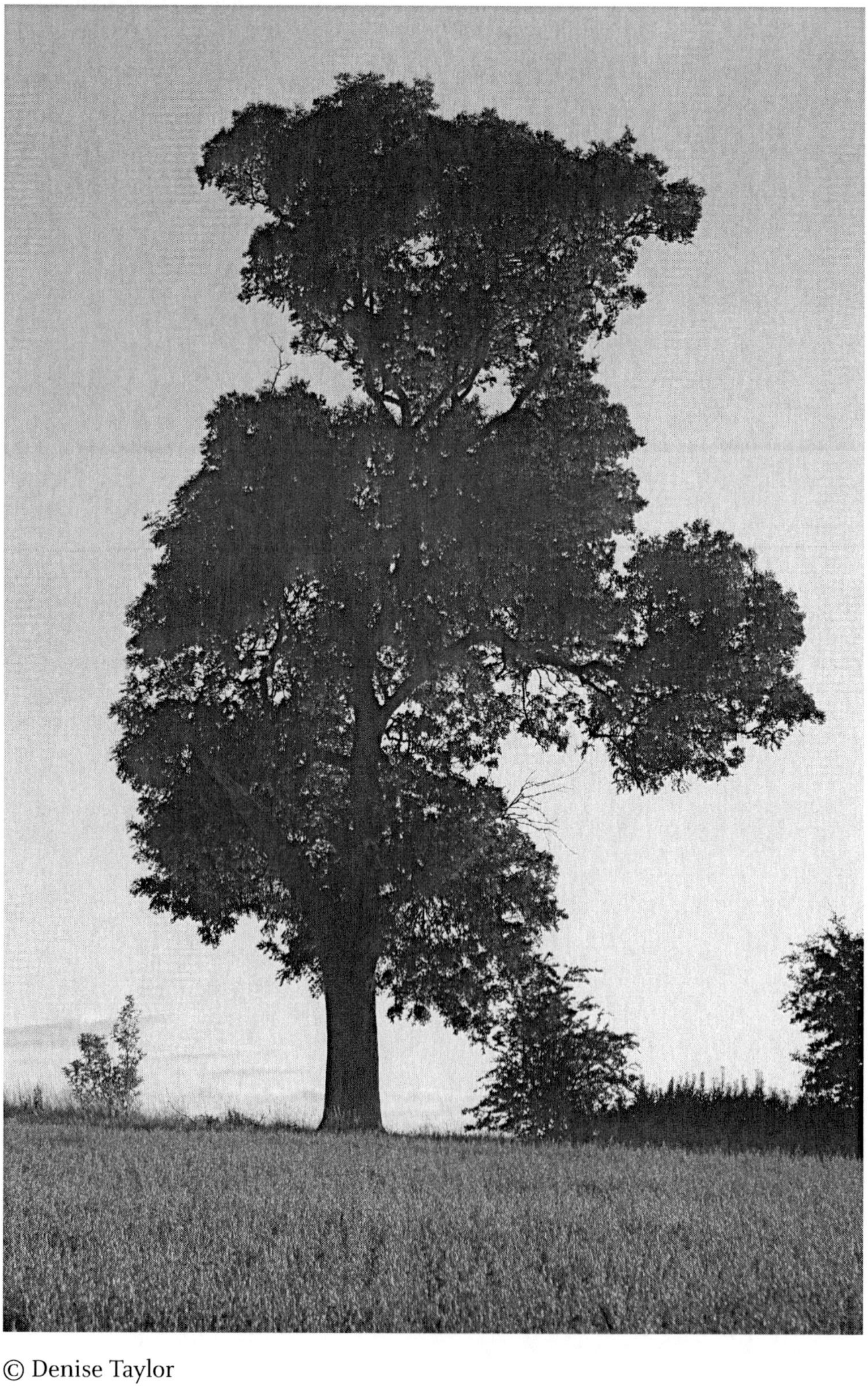

© Denise Taylor

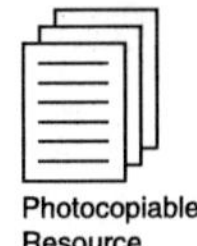

Photocopiable Resource 17

Some Examples of Moral Dilemmas

A fisherman and his wife live on a small island. Their family has lived there for many generations, and fishing is their tradition. It is the only life they know. His father was a fisherman, his grandfather, his father before him, and so on. The fisherman and his wife have five small children. He works hard every day to catch enough fish to feed his growing family. Any surplus fish he catches, he sells at the market on the mainland. Just lately he has been catching fewer and fewer fish, and has noticed that there are more seals in the area than there were before. He believes they are eating all the fish. If the fisherman isn't able to catch more fish his family will go hungry, and they will not have enough money to live on. He decides that his only course of action is to get his gun and kill as many seals as he can so that he will have more fish to catch himself.

Many people think that wearing fur is no longer acceptable in a civilized society. Yet we wear leather and eat meat. Should people be allowed to wear fur if they choose to? Why/why not?

A friend is having some problems at home and he has some homework that needs to be handed in tomorrow. You have some time spare and you really want to help your friend out. Should you do his homework for him? Why/why not?

A friend borrowed some paints from the art department without asking permission so that she could finish some work at home. She has forgotten to return them and the Head Teacher announced in assembly that some paints have been stolen, and she is going to find out who took them. Your friend asks you to cover up for her. What should you do?

You are in Year 5, and someone in your class is being bullied by a group of older children in Year 6. They have confided in you about the bullying and they don't know what to do. The group of older children have said that if you tell anyone about what has happened, then you will be their next victim. What should you do?

You buy a magazine from the local shop. The assistant gives you your change and outside the shop you discover that she has given you £2 too much. Should you keep the money, or should you go back into the shop and give the money back?

CHAPTER

8 Knowledge and Truth

It is through our senses that we learn about the world. Without our senses, there would be no way for information about the external world to reach our minds and be experienced.

We do not know something is true because an expert tells us so. We should be able to check it for ourselves using our own sense experience. Of course, we do, for convenience, often rely on the 'expertise' of others. Similarly, we cannot entirely rely on intuition. Our intuition may be correct, especially if we have unconsciously noticed things, but again we have to be able to check it against experience.

Experience and logical reason are thus the primary (main) sources of knowledge. Secondary sources should be used with caution, and secondary sources of information should be open to question.

Explain to the Children

- We must have good reason based on strong evidence to say that we **know** something, and even then we may be wrong.
- We can only know things if they are true. We cannot **know** false things, we can only believe these.
- We try to get at the truth by acquiring stronger evidence and better reasons for what we will accept as the truth.

Skills

- The children should be introduced to epistemology as part of the introduction to philosophy.
- They should understand that it is only with strong evidence that we are justified in considering that we have knowledge.
- They need to recognize experience and logical thought as the primary sources of knowledge.
- Secondary sources of knowledge such as the word of an 'authority' or our own intuition should be open to question.

Preliminaries to the Story and Vocabulary

The story, *Mary Mary Quite Contrary*, encapsulates a key philosophical problem in the human quest for truth and certainty. How can we know the world as it is in itself since we apprehend it through our particular human sense organs and then interpret our sense impressions through human concepts which have been constructed to serve human needs and interests? Can what is true ever be known? How can we trust our senses and our concepts? Perhaps they distort the world as it truly is, just as the glasses which Mary puts on distort what she sees.

Vocabulary	
Mama	Mother
Papa	Father
Babula	Grandma (in Polish)
Contrary	opposite
Shrugged	shook her shoulders showing she didn't care
Spectacles	(eye) glasses
Transparent	see-through
Waver	move unsteadily back and forth
Blur	smudge, become unclear
Shriek	scream
Weird	odd, strange
Misjudging	estimating wrongly
Desperately	in despair, in great distress
Spiky	sharply pointed
Nasty	unpleasant

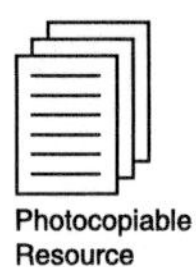

Mary Mary Quite Contrary

Mary Mary Quite Contrary

'Tea's ready Mary,' called Mama. Mary was in the garden.

'I don't want any,' said Mary. 'I'm playing with Adam and I don't want to come in.'

'Now don't let it go cold,' said Papa, appearing at the back doorway. 'Come in now please.'

'No,' said Mary. 'After we've finished our game.' Papa sighed and shook his head.

'She needs a good slap,' Mary heard her Babula say to Papa. But Mary knew her Papa would never do that.

'She's well named is that child,' Babula went on. 'Mary, Mary quite contrary. She never does what anyone wants her to.'

Mary shrugged and turned back to little Adam, who was only three and lived next door.

Later, when Mary did go into tea, it was cold of course.

'Urgh,' she said, pushing her plate away and Mama heated it up in the microwave. Babula sighed.

'You should make her eat it cold,' she said.

The next day Mary's Uncle Stefan came to stay. 'I'll soon cure our Miss Contrary,' he said.

'Oh no you won't,' Mary said.

'Now don't you touch my things,' said Uncle Stefan, 'especially these spectacles.'

The spectacles were big with round green glass set in thick black rubber rims. They were on the coffee table where Uncle Stefan had left them. Mary put them on. They were surprisingly light. Another surprising thing was that the green glass did not make everything look green. However, things started to change a little. Some things became almost transparent, as if the glasses were X-ray glasses. Other things began to waver and blur as though the glasses had water in the lenses. Colours changed and some colours even seemed to disappear. Green things and blue all looked the same, a sort of Grue.

'I told you not to touch my glasses,' said Uncle Stefan, coming in from the garden.

Photocopiable Resource

At that moment a wild fur covered creature with sharp teeth ran into the room too. Mary gave a shriek, before, half a second later, she realized it was only a cat. *It's these glasses,* Mary thought. *They change everything. It's weird.*

Mary hated the glasses. She tried to take them off but somehow her arm kept misjudging the distance to her face and she couldn't manage to remove them. She tried several times.

'Uncle Stefan,' she said, 'take your glasses off me.'

Uncle Stefan moved his head back and forth. That looked weird too. 'No,' he said.

'No!' exclaimed Mary. 'Why not? You didn't want me to wear them in the first place.'

'They might teach you a lesson Mary,' said Uncle Stefan. 'You can see what it's like when someone won't do what you want.'

All that day Mary tried to get the glasses off her face. She tried to lift them off. She tried to shake them off. She even tried to knock them off by moving her head against the corner of the sideboard. Somehow the glasses wouldn't allow her to judge the distances correctly. She went into the kitchen in search of her Mama.

'Mama, could you please take these glasses off for me? Somehow I can't manage it myself,' Mary said.

'No dear,' Mama said, and she didn't even turn round.

'Please Mama,' Mary pleaded. Mama simply carried on cooking the tea. Mary couldn't believe it. Mama had never let her down before. Mary went into the garden in search of her Papa.

No sooner had Mary stepped out of the doorway than she saw a snake by her feet. Her heart squeezed painfully in her chest before she realized it was only the broom handle. Tentatively she stepped over it, to be confronted by a towering giant. She froze in fear before she realized it was only the tree. These spectacles were making the garden a very strange and scary place to be. Frightened, Mary turned to go back into the house but she couldn't aim herself in the right direction. She blinked back hot tears. Mary wanted everything to be back to normal and no one would help her. What could she do?

Mary thought of Adam. He would help her. She knew that with these glasses on she couldn't get to his house. Perhaps she could call him and he would hear. 'Adam,' she shouted desperately. 'Adam.' And suddenly there he was. He'd climbed over the wall between his garden and hers.

'Hi Mary,' he said.

His spiky red hair looked, through the glasses, as though it were on fire.

'What funny glasses Mary,' Adam said.

'Yes. Lift them off me please, dear Adam,' Mary said, and Adam, ever ready to help his friend, reached forward and removed the glasses from her face. What a relief! Mary looked round the garden. She really enjoyed seeing the world as it should be. She also saw, with alarm, that Adam had put on the glasses. But he didn't seem to be scared. He was laughing.

'They're trick glasses Mary! Trick glasses!'

Gently Mary lifted them from his face. 'Yes, they are trick glasses Adam,' she said, 'but not very nice ones. I'll give them back to Uncle Stefan.'

'Will you play with me Mary?' Adam asked.

'Yes Adam. You're my super hero. You rescued me from these nasty glasses.'

Adam was grinning.

'I'm a super hero,' he said, sounding pleased.

Uncle Stefan came into the garden.

Mary held out the spectacles. 'Your glasses, Uncle Stefan. I'm sorry I took them.'

'That's OK Mary,' he said, taking them back. 'You've got to come into tea now.'

Mary was just about to say no but somehow she didn't want to.

'Sure,' she said instead. 'I'll see you later Adam,' and she followed Uncle Stefan into the house for her tea.

Talking About the Story

Ask the Children

- Why did Mary's grandma call Mary **contrary**?
- How did Uncle Stefan intend to teach Mary a lesson and cure her of being contrary?
- Why did Mary put Uncle Stefan's spectacles on?
- Why didn't Mary take off the spectacles?

Points for Discussion

- Why do you think that sometimes we want to do the very thing we are told not to do?
- Do you think we can ever know anything for certain, or might we always be wrong (like looking through trick glasses)?
- What is the difference between **knowing** something and merely **believing** something? (What we believe may or may not be true but knowledge implies truth.)
- What do we mean when we say something is true?
- Grue is an example that has been used in philosophical discussion. If we could not tell the difference between blue and green we would see these colours as the same. We could call the colour we saw **grue**. How do I know that you see colours as I see colours?

Cross-curricular Story Activities

Key Stage 1 Activity

Let the children draw a picture of Mary in the garden in shades of one colour. They can choose the colour they will use – black, red, blue or green. Now they draw the same picture in full colour. Let them see and discuss the difference between the full colour picture and the monochrome one.

Key Stage 2 Activity

Let the children do the picture activity described above (for KS1). In addition, the children can discuss in what ways the choice of different mono-colours makes a difference to the atmosphere or feel of the pictures.

For Enthusiastic or Gifted Children

Give each of the children a copy of the story illustration. See how the magic glasses have turned the cat into a tiger and the broom handle into a snake. Let them imagine looking round a garden wearing these glasses. They write a page about what they see. What other things change in interesting or scary ways?

Critical Thinking Activities

Key Stage 1 Activities

KS1 Activity 1: Puzzles

Give the children a copy of the photograph on page 117 (*Photocopiable Resource 18*). The girl in the photograph is looking puzzled (not scared as Mary was). Discuss what things in the garden might puzzle her. For example, what creature made the tracks across the soil? Why is grass green? Why are there no flowers growing under the tree? Ask the children what things puzzle them, and discuss these.

KS1 Activity 2: True or False?

Let the children puzzle out which sentences on page 118 (*Photocopiable Resource 19*) are true and which are false. (For some they might want to write 'maybe'.) They can then write true or false in the blank lines. Finally, have a class discussion about the children's answers.

Key Stage 2 Activities

KS2 Activity 1: Justified Belief

Get the children to think up some statements that they believe, e.g. this pencil is blue; my friend's name is Mary; one and one is two; we should not tell lies, etc.

Write these on the board. Now have a class discussion about each statement. Is it justified (by evidence or by argument)? How certain is it? Could we consider it to be knowledge (i.e. known to be true)?

KS2 Activity 2: Science Fiction

Science fiction can be a good way of showing children how other creatures or aliens might sense things in a different way and live differently in a different world. You could read a selection of science fiction stories with this alternative theme and then have the children create their own aliens on another planet. They could go on to write their own story about their alien.

For Enthusiastic or Gifted Children

Imagine that Uncle Stefan's glasses showed the world as it really is. Without the glasses we see a distorted world! The children write their own story called *Uncle Stefan's Hat*. In the story, the hero or heroine enters an alternative world when he or she wears the hat.

Photocopiable Resource 18

The Girl in the Heart-shaped Glasses

Photocopiable Resource 19

True or False (The Girl in the Heart-shaped Glasses)

	True / False / Maybe
The girl in the picture is wearing glasses	______
The child in the picture is a girl	______
Her glasses are an unusual shape	______
We know that she likes her glasses	______
The girl is in a garden	______
The girl is looking puzzled	______
The girl is happy	______
The girl is wearing a zip-up jacket	______
The girl is alone in the garden	______

Interdisciplinary Project on Gardens and Gardening

Give the children a copy of the story photograph showing Mary in the spectacles. She's looking puzzled. What is she asking herself? Can the children think of different subject questions? A science question, a history question, a geography question, an artistic/aesthetic question.

Gardens make a useful topic for an interdisciplinary project. (Perhaps the children could also do some practical work in the school garden or through growing their own plants in the classroom.)

Science

The children could find out more about plants.

English/History

Do the children know the nursery rhyme *Mary Mary Quite Contrary*?

Mary Mary Quite Contrary

Mary Mary quite contrary,
How does your garden grow?
With silver bells and cockle shells,
And pretty maids all in a row.

KS1 children will enjoy reading and reciting nursery rhymes and KS2 children will be interested to know the meaning and derivation of some of these old verses.

Geography

The children could learn about the different flora across the globe, and how the biomes affect these, for example the trees and plants in tropical rainforests compared with the trees and plants in arboreal forests or deserts.

Values

Environmental concerns – there are numerous concerns about the environment including climate change, the rate of species extinction, air and water pollution, and so on. Often the conflict in values arises from our differing viewpoints, usually concerned with ecology versus economy.

Philosophical/Spiritual Discussion

Give the children the *Photocopiable Resource 20* from page 121. Read the garden story with the children as a way into discussion about the existence of the gardener (and God). Do they think there was a gardener who created and designed the garden? Do they think that there is a God who created and designed our world and the universe?

Photocopiable Resource 20

The Woodland Gardener

One day a brother and sister were playing in a local wood. Sunlight streamed through the trees and the children were enjoying themselves. They played jumping the stream. They played hide and seek in the trees. They searched for conkers and fir cones. Suddenly, to their surprise, they came into a large, treeless space among the trees.

'What a lovely garden', said the sister. 'I wonder who made it'.

'No one', said her brother. 'It just grew here by itself'.

'No. There must have been a gardener to plant the garden. Look at the way those flowers make a picture of a butterfly!'

'I think they grew like that by chance. They have grown in a way that looks like a plan but that's an illusion. They just grew like that'.

'But someone must have looked after the plants and weeded the garden'.

The brother and sister could not agree, and they decided to come back to the woodland garden every week. The sister was sure that one day they would find the gardener at work there. The brother was equally sure that there was no gardener and that the natural garden would soon be overgrown, like the rest of the wood.

They continued to visit for a long time. They never met a gardener but the garden continued to flourish. After each visit the brother and sister continued to disagree.

'How can there be a gardener we never see?' asked the brother.

'Well, why should the garden continue to exist without him?' said the sister.

They have never agreed from that day to this.

CHAPTER

9 Knowledge as Worthwhile Learning

Education is concerned with the development of knowledge and understanding. Thus knowledge is an important aspect of education. However, not just any knowledge is part of education. It needs to be **worthwhile** knowledge. This is why what we count as education reveals our values – reveals what we count as worthwhile. The National Curriculum is based on the subjects/forms of knowledge which our society deem to be worthwhile. Philosophers have suggested that knowledge is split into different kinds, each of which has its own key concepts, truth criteria and methods of enquiry. For example, key concepts in science include space, time, object, mass; in religion key concepts include God, faith, spiritual; and key concepts in English/language include communication and meaning. However, philosophical reflection can be applied to all these concepts i.e. applied in all forms of knowledge and thus in all areas of the National Curriculum.

Explain to the Children

- Critical thinking should be applied right across the curriculum, i.e. in all subjects.
- In all subjects learn to ask questions and to look down on (analyse) the material.
- Education is about worthwhile knowledge (ask the children for examples). Some knowledge is not education because it is not worthwhile. For example, learning how to be a pickpocket is not education because it is immoral. (You could ask the children for some more examples of knowledge which is not education, because it is not worthwhile.)

Skills

- The children should be able to approach all subject areas critically.
- The children should learn to recognize the difference between what counts as a good reason in the different areas. Thus, in science a good reason is one based in evidence from observation and experience. A good moral reason will be based on considerations of fairness and kindness to others (justice and care). In music, art, literature they will learn to make relevant aesthetic judgements.

Preliminaries to the Story and Vocabulary

This story touches on some of the areas of more traditional knowledge that in a modern society we may perhaps have lost. Both Tom and Eva's Mum have gained a lot of knowledge through observation and learning over a period of time, and they are both passing this knowledge on to Eva. It is through Tom's wider knowledge of the landscape that he is able to deduce that the cause of the problem of the disappearing forest creatures is something that must be affecting all of them, and so he and Eva set off on a quest to find out what that might be. Tom already suspects it might be the water source that is the problem, and he tests his theory.

Part of the point of this story is that sometimes knowledge about particular subjects can be insular, and, for whatever reason, we neglect to take a more holistic approach towards cause and effect. In the story, the slash and burn policy upriver, and the pollution from the rubbish dump, may appear not to be related to the disappearance downriver of the animals in the forest. We therefore need to question knowledge and our underlying assumptions, and try to be more open-minded in our thinking in order that the knowledge we acquire is not only worthwhile but as complete as it can be.

Vocabulary

Disappeared	vanished from sight
Unusual	not usual, common or ordinary
Chatter	a succession of quick, non-speechlike sounds such as made by birds or monkeys
Elders	people older or higher in rank; influential members of a tribe or community
Miracle	a wonder or marvel that is beyond belief
Woodsman	a person experienced and skilled in the arts of the woods
Pole-lathe	a machine used for working wood and metal that holds the material and rotates it above a horizontal axis against a tool that shapes it
Flute	a musical instrument consisting of a tube with a series of finger holes or keys
Wise	having knowledge and information; being able to use knowledge and information in a discerning way
Medicine	a substance or substances used to treat illness or disease
Heal	make well or better
Potions	drinks or drafts said to have medicinal properties (and sometimes poisonous properties)
Lotions	ointment or creams used to treat skin complaints
Expedition	an excursion, journey or voyage for some specific purpose

Rustling	to make soft sounds by moving or stirring something such as leaves, silk material or paper
Investigation	a search inquiry to establish facts; a detailed or careful examination
Delegation	a group or body of delegates chosen to represent a unit or body
Suspected	believed to be the case or to be likely or probable; surmised
Sediment	mineral or organic matter deposited in a river or body of water

Photocopiable Resource

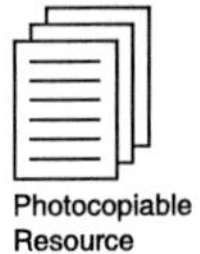

The Silent Forest

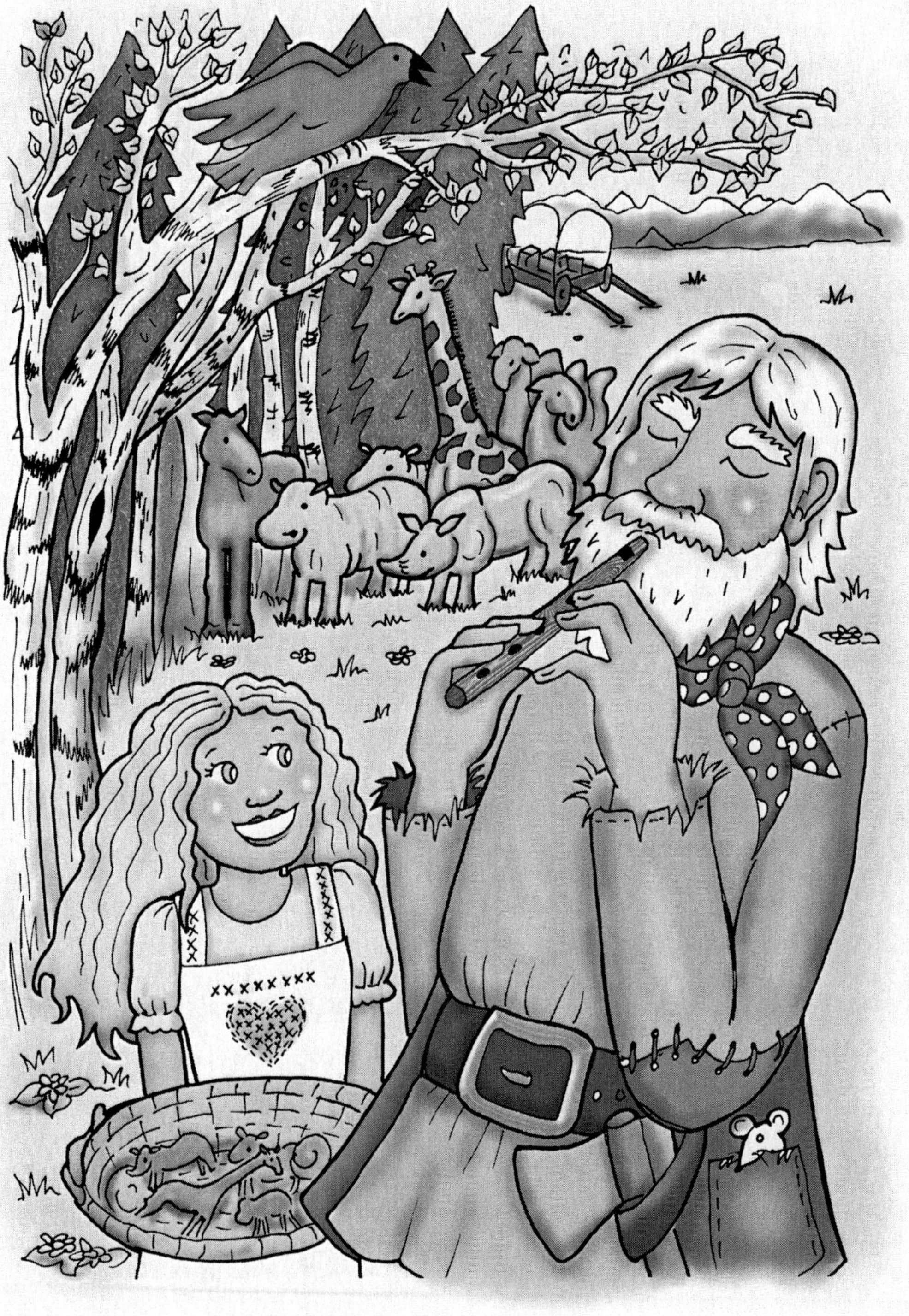

The Silent Forest

Something very strange has been happening in our forest just lately. All the creatures disappeared. They just vanished and nobody knows where they went to. Everyone in the town agreed that something must be done, but no one could decide what. It was all very unusual. And very sad, because I really missed the chatter of the blackbirds. They sound just like they're telling each other off, and it always makes me smile. I hadn't heard the foxes barking at night either. It was very quiet. Too quiet! Not even the rat-a-tat-tat of the woodpecker high up in the trees.

The town elders kept meeting to discuss the problem, but no one could find out what had happened to all the animals. Why would they just suddenly disappear like that?

It had been almost a week and still there had been no sight of a deer, badger, fox, rabbit, squirrel, hedgehog, woodpecker, raven, song thrush, blackbird, mole or even a mouse.

Anyway, like a miracle, Tom turned up. He's a travelling woodsman and makes the most amazing things you've ever seen. He has a machine that he calls a pole-lathe and lots of different knives and chisels. He calls himself a turner. He says it sounds better. More important.

Last year when he came to stay in town he made me the most gorgeous flute. It doesn't make a sound like an ordinary flute, but when I play it in the forest, all the little creatures come to see me to listen to the beautiful music that only they can hear. I only play it though when no one else is around, otherwise the creatures won't come. They are afraid of other people, but somehow they seem to know I won't hurt them.

Tom was really concerned when I told him that the animals in the forest had all disappeared. And he wanted to help me to find them straight away. I told him that I could use my flute to call them back, but he said that this probably wouldn't work right now. There was a reason all the animals had gone away, and he said that we must first of all find the reason.

Tom is very wise. He knows the names of all the animals and all the trees and plants, and he's been teaching me. My Mum is good at remembering the names of plants too and she knows which plants we can eat in the forest, and which we can use to make medicines. I want to be like Mum and Tom when I grow up and be able to heal people with potions and lotions made from roots, leaves and berries.

Tom went to meet with the town elders straight away to discuss the mystery of the disappearing animals, and later he came to fetch me. I was helping Mum to bake some bread, but she agreed that I could go with Tom on an expedition into the forest. She put some food in a basket for us, and we set off.

I couldn't believe how quiet the forest was. The only sound was the rustling of the leaves in the trees, but after walking for a while we heard the sound of water rushing over rocks and stones. As soon as he heard it, Tom wanted to go to the river. He said it was just what we were looking for, but I didn't understand yet why.

The river looked horrible. It was all brown and yucky, and didn't look good at all. In fact it looked very ill. If a river can look ill, of course, which I think it can now that I've seen this one.

The sight of the river concerned Tom. He frowned and looked quite angry too. He said that this is what was causing the problem. All the creatures of the forest need to drink water, and if the water was bad, then they would have to go somewhere else to find good water. That's why they had disappeared!

That made perfect sense to me, but what was causing the river to go bad? Tom said this would take a little more investigation, but at least we now knew that the problem was the river, and so we headed back to town and Tom went off to tell the elders what we had discovered.

The next day, the elders gathered everyone together, and after a lot of discussion it was decided that the town should send a delegation upriver to find out what was going on. Tom led the delegation and this time I had to stay at home. I was really disappointed, but I helped Mum to do the chores, and we were

very busy gathering more herbs for some new potions she was making. Mum taught me the names of some plants I didn't know, and what they could be used for.

Tom and the delegation came back a few days later and it turned out that, as he suspected, the problem lies farther up the river in the next town. Apparently they have something called a 'slash and burn' policy. I didn't understand this at first, but Tom explained it to me. He said it's where they cut down the forest and burn everything to clear the land ready to plant crops. Over time this causes sediment to build up in the river, which is not always a good thing, and can cause problems downstream. But on top of all that, the town upriver had also put their rubbish dump near a bend in the river, and the heavy rains over the winter had made bad stuff from the rubbish leak into the river.

Tom and the delegation were sent back to the town to discuss the problem, and the elders in the other town agreed to move the dump, and to clear the river of all the sediment.

Everyone was relieved that we had found the cause of the problem and they were really grateful to Tom for helping them to solve the mystery. The whole town celebrated, and Tom played one of his flutes, which was one that made proper music.

Two weeks later, the river started to run clear again, and Tom said that now was the time to go and play my flute in the forest. He came with me. It was a beautifully sunny day, and we stood in a small glade by the river. I played and played my magic flute all afternoon, and I was getting very tired. I was about to give up when all of a sudden we heard a rustling noise, and a large hare appeared from the undergrowth. It hopped into the glade and was quickly followed by the cutest little fawn I have ever seen. Soon other creatures began to appear.

I jumped up and down with happiness, and hugged Tom. 'You are the cleverest man in the world,' I told him.

Talking about the Story

Ask the Children

- Why was the forest so silent?
- What did Tom make with his pole-lathe?
- What made the creatures disappear from the forest?
- Why was Eva's flute magic?
- Why do you think the polluted river affected all the creatures?
- What did Eva learn from her mother and Tom?

Points for Discussion

- Are traditional forms of knowledge worthwhile knowledge? We have lost many of our ancient skills and customs, much of it as a result of progress and technological advancements, but there are some who question this and think that some of the knowledge we have lost has been very valuable and worthwhile knowledge.
- There is worthwhile knowledge in the subjects that you study at school. Which of these subjects do you think have worthwhile knowledge? Why/why not?
- In the story, Eva learns from her mother and Tom. They pass on their knowledge to her. What other ways are there of acquiring knowledge? Discuss this with the children.

Cross-curricular Story Activities

Key Stage 1 Activity

Using a large sheet of paper, or several sheets of paper, create a basic forest or woodland scene that the children can populate with different animals and plants that they can either draw or paint or cut from magazines. Try to include as many plants and animals as possible so that the children can see the wonderful biodiversity that exists in our woodlands. Use the collage for further class work about the different species. What are the names of the plants and animals? Can they be grouped or organized into different categories? Where do they live? What do they eat? Are they eaten by other creatures? Are they poisonous? What sounds do they make? How long do they live? How big or small are they? How big or small are they compared to other plants and animals?

Key Stage 2 Activity

Using a combination of primary and secondary sources of knowledge, ask the children to write a story about a walk in a forest or a wooded park. Encourage the children to describe what they see, hear, smell, feel and perhaps taste. They could perhaps imagine that they are one of the creatures in the forest such as a deer, a badger or a fox. How do these creatures experience the forest and what knowledge do they need to survive?

Critical Thinking Activities

About Knowledge

- **What Knowledge is**. There is no one definition, but it is generally agreed that knowledge is the expertise and skills acquired by a person through experience or education. The definition of knowledge in philosophy is still an ongoing debate, but the classical definition is that for there to be knowledge at least three criteria must be fulfilled. Thus to count as knowledge a statement must be justified, true and believed.
- **Types of Knowledge**. Knowledge can be categorized in a number of different ways, but for the purpose of this chapter, we will outline four types:
    - *Received Knowledge*: Knowledge as objective facts, information and right answers acquired from an authority.
    - *Subjective Knowledge*: Knowledge based on subjective experience where the truth may not be known, and there may be differences of opinion. However, when the facts are not known one particular theory may be as good as another as long as it makes sense.
    - *Procedural Knowledge*: Knowledge is neither facts and right answers, nor is it a matter of opinion. This gives rise to complexity and the need for evidence to support knowledge statements. This type of knowledge uses scientific and systematic methods of analysis to obtain evidence, and involves looking at things from different perspectives, and by experimentation.
    - *Constructed Knowledge*: Knowledge as critically informed intersection of facts, experience and methods. It recognizes the complexities of knowledge and that although contextual, relative and uncertain, it is possible to form opinions and make commitments to one's stance or position. This is the type of knowledge that helps us to form our worldviews while at the same time acknowledging the uncertainty and the need to constantly evaluate and review one's assumptions and beliefs about the knowledge acquired.
- **How We Acquire Knowledge**. Knowledge is acquired through experience and through education, and is an ongoing and lifelong process. Although knowledge is acquired from essentially two sources (see below), the way in which we access information and data

(i.e. evidence, and thus some may say some of our knowledge) has changed dramatically throughout the centuries. Oral traditions were replaced by texts and written materials after the invention of the Gutenberg press, and in modern times we access information across multiple media platforms such as the Internet, television and film, audio, and other electronic media. In the Age of Information, it is probably even more important to question the information we access and check that the sources are reliable and credible.

(Note: as technology continues to advance and develop, we will be presented with even more ways of accessing information and different ways of learning. For example, virtual learning environments and serious games (games that are for more than just entertainment) are already starting to offer new and different ways of learning that will challenge our sensory perceptions and the way we view the world.

- **Sources of Knowledge**. There are two sources of knowledge: primary and secondary. Primary knowledge is the knowledge we acquire or experience first-hand through our five senses or through reason, logic and evidence. Secondary knowledge comes from external sources such as an authority or through intuition. These sources of knowledge may be good sources, but critical thinking skills and judgement should be used to establish the validity and credibility of secondary sources.

Critical thinking skills help us to understand what is worthwhile knowledge and what is not worthwhile.

Acquiring Primary Knowledge

Primary knowledge is gained through sense experience, and through our observations of, and experiences in the world. Acquiring primary knowledge is an integral part of the day-to-day activities in the classroom. Children are busy observing, experimenting and using all their senses to gain an understanding of the subjects and topics they are studying.

Use some of the exercises in this chapter, and throughout the rest of this book, as a basis for discussing with the children what they are learning from the perspective of acquiring knowledge. Many of the exercises use the critical thinking skills discussed throughout this book, and in particular how children approach a topic through asking questions and using their research skills and tools.

Key Stage 1 Activities

KS1 Activity 1: Primary Knowledge – Observation

Exercises using all the senses can be fun as well as educative. The children could make good use of the outdoor classroom space in particular, or perhaps a visit to the local park or nature reserve could be arranged. Even a very basic exercise such as asking the children to close their eyes in an outdoor setting for a few minutes and then asking them to describe how many different sounds they can hear heightens their awareness of sensory perception.

Observations and experiments can be carried out in an outdoor setting, counting the numbers of plants or animals in a defined area or space, or conducting experiments about the weather using simple measuring equipment.

Set aside time after each activity to discuss what the children have learned, and the methods they have used.

KS1 Activity 2: Primary Knowledge – Sensory Perception and Awareness

Synesthesia is a neurogically based condition where the use of one sense involuntarily affects another sense. For example, some people report that they see bright and vivid colours when they hear certain sounds. Using the exercise above where the children have been asked to describe the sounds they hear when they have their eyes closed, ask the children to describe the colour they see when hearing particular sounds. They could then paint a picture, or create a digital picture on the computer, expressing the sounds they have heard as art.

Key Stage 2 Activities

KS2 Activity 1: Primary Knowledge – Observation

For KS2 children, use similar methods outlined in this section for KS1, but in addition, ask the KS2 children to record their observations more formally using an Observation Diary or Journal. There are many observation activities that the children can undertake. Below are some examples:

1. Moon phases – to be carried out over a period of at least one week, but ideally over the period of a full moon cycle. Ask the children to record the moon phases each day in their journal, and add a sketch of the moon on that particular day. The children can choose to record other interesting and relevant information, and may also want to explore other scientific aspects such as the moon's gravitational influence on tides, etc. As an extension to this activity, the children could research myths and legends about the moon and write their own stories.
2. Obtain an ant farm for the class, and using a journal or log and other observational methods such as photographs and films, observe and record the daily lives and activities of the ants over a period of time.
3. In an outdoor classroom setting, there are many opportunities for observing the natural world through all our senses. By using their critical thinking skills, the

children could carry out basic research into a variety of life cycles and natural processes. This could include observing creatures in their habitats and recording their findings, or growing plants of their own and experimenting with this, e.g. how well a plant grows in the shade compared to an open, sunny spot.

4. Cooking is another ideal activity to enable children to practise some of their critical thinking skills (see Learning to Cook photograph on page 134, *Photocopiable Resource 21*). Cooking involves research activity (for example, finding recipes and sourcing ingredients), observation, using the senses, exercising judgement. Food is also such an important part of cultural and social activity that extension activities can easily be incorporated into cooking (for example, researching the different cultural approaches to growing, eating and sharing our food). The moral and ethical dimensions can also be covered when discussing issues such as food miles, GM foods, the treatment of farmed animals, etc.

KS2 Activity 2: Primary Knowledge – Sensory Perception and Awareness

Synesthesia is a neurogically based condition where the use of one sense involuntarily affects another sense. For example, some people report that they see bright and vivid colours when they hear certain sounds.

If the school IT and Media Suite has sufficient resources, KS2 children could extend the KS1 activity by collecting natural and found sounds in an outdoor classroom setting using simple recording equipment. The children can then create a piece of visual digital art using the software available, for example, creating visual images that represent different bird songs. If the school does not have audio/visual software available, open source software for editing music and digital audio recordings are easily accessible on the Internet.

The aim of these activities is the acquisition of primary knowledge through observation and sensory awareness and perception.

KS2 Activity 3: Reasoning

Using reasoning and logical thinking is another way of acquiring knowledge. Conundrums and exercises in logical thinking are an excellent way of practising reasoning skills.

An Example: Where are the Fish?

Two fathers and two sons are on a fishing trip. They catch one fish each. No fish were thrown back. There are three fish in the boat. How is this possible? (Answer: The men were a son, his father and his grandfather.)

Photocopiable
Resource

Photocopiable Resource 21

Learning to Cook

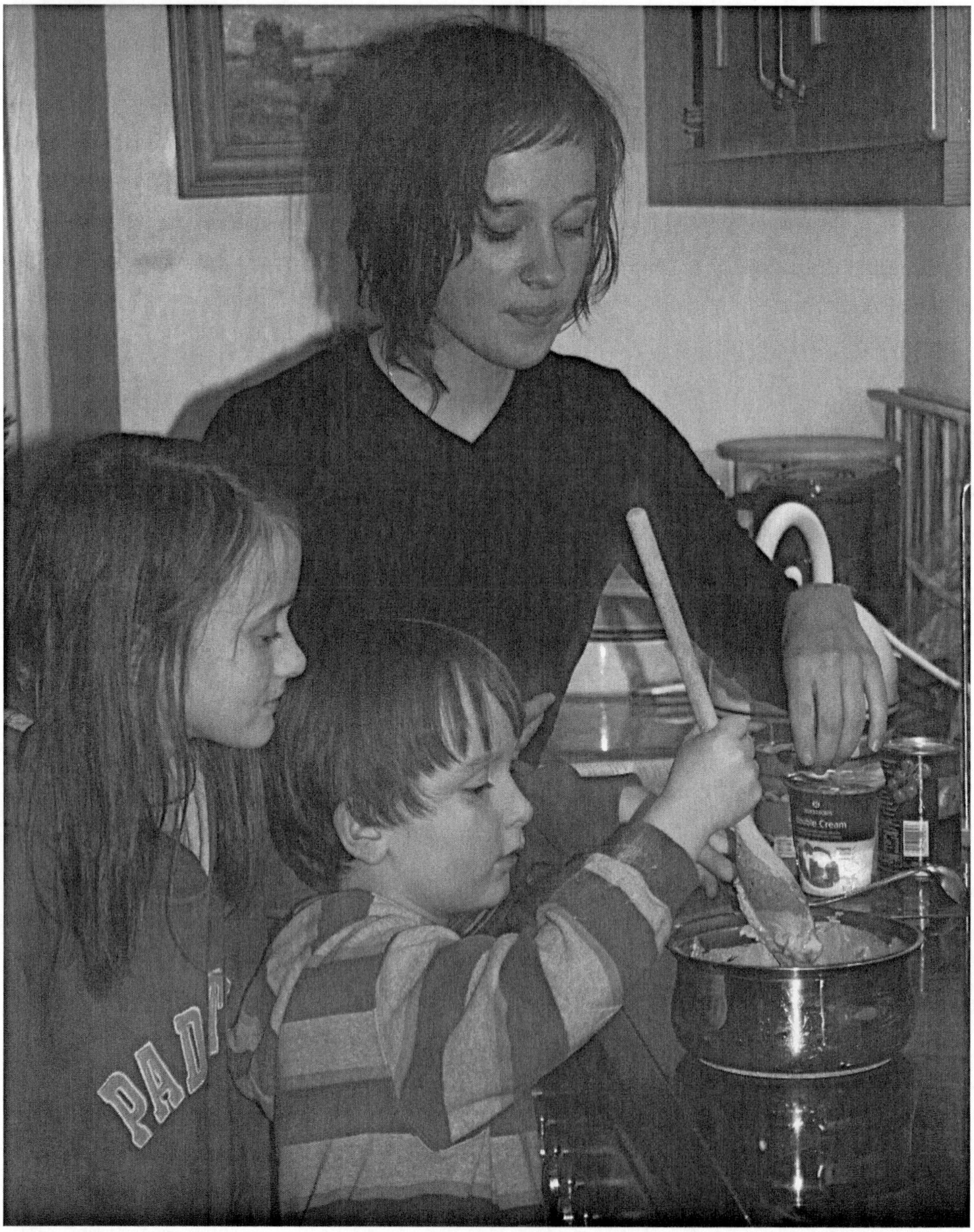

Learning to cook is one of the most enjoyable activities where knowledge can be developed on many different levels. All the senses are used, and children require good observation skills. Children can also conduct experiments when cooking.

CHAPTER

10 The Problem of Perception

Our perception of the external world is a primary source of knowledge. However, philosophers have questioned the reliability of perception. Their concerns have included that what we perceive is partly dependent on our sense organs. If these were different we would perceive the world differently (some would claim this would be to live in a different world). In addition, we sometimes have illusions, perceptual errors and ambiguities, vivid dreams and hallucinations. How can we be sure of the reliability of any given perception? This is what philosophers mean by the 'problem of perception'.

These concerns about perception connect with metaphysical and epistemological questions. How can we know what there is, and how can we obtain knowledge of the world if we cannot rely on our perceptions? And if we cannot rely on our perceptions, we cannot trust our own experience or rely on the scientific method of observation and experiment! Thus the problem of perception is an important philosophical problem.

Explain to the Children

- Explain that we can only learn about the world through our perceptions of it – what we see, hear, smell, taste, touch.
- If our sense organs were different, we would perceive the world differently. We can understand this by thinking about other creatures. The swan on page 50 perceives his reflection as another swan. Non-human creatures cannot interpret reflected images. Some creatures, such as bats, dolphins and whales, 'see' the world through sound, using sonar and echo location to find prey and to establish where they are.
- We have all experienced illusions (ask the children to give some examples). In these cases we have made a mistake about what we have seen or heard.
- If we may have made a mistake, how can we rely on our perceptions? This is called the problem of perception.

Skills

- To understand the problem of perception.
- To be able to think of appropriate (rational) ways of checking perceptions that may be mistaken.

Preliminaries to the Story and Vocabulary

The problem of perception is a key problem in philosophy and one that children can understand and find fascinating. It is a key problem because it is central to ontology, metaphysics and epistemology. It is fascinating to children because (probably for the first time) these ideas shake their taken-for-granted world upside down. Suppose this present classroom is only really a vivid dream? Suppose I don't see colours or feel pain in the same way as everyone else? How do I know I'm seeing my friend like everyone else does? Maybe he's a friendly alien? Obviously one wants to interest and perhaps amuse the children – not frighten them! In the story in Chapter 8, Mary is alarmed rather than really frightened, but she does experience the problem of perception in a very direct way! In *Daisy Chains*, the heroine, Daisy, experiences the problem of perception in the form of trying to distinguish between dream and reality.

Vocabulary	
Favourite	the one you like best
Charm bracelet	a bracelet with little charms attached to it
Picking	plucking
Promised	vowed to do something. If you don't keep a promise it is a kind of lie. You have let someone down.
Special occasions	a social event such as a party or other celebration
Clue	a piece of evidence that helps you work out what has happened
Linking	joining
Stalk	the green stem of a flower
Reluctantly	unwillingly
Glittery	little points of light shining on the object
Admired	liked very much
Thread	thin piece of the flower stalk – thin as cotton thread

Daisy Chains

Photocopiable Resource

Daisy Chains

Daisy was unhappy. She had lost her favourite bracelet. Her charm bracelet. She had been sitting on the grass in the garden and making a daisy chain. She had made a small slit with her nail near the head of the last daisy in the chain and threaded the next one through. Seven daisies were linked by their stalks. She had wrapped these around her wrist like a bracelet and had given a gasp of dismay. Her silver charm bracelet had gone. Daisy had been given a silver charm to add to her bracelet every birthday and Christmas. She could never decide which one she liked best; the book that really opened perhaps, or the silver teddy bear with the smiling face.

'Mum,' she wailed through the open window. 'I've lost my bracelet. My silver bracelet.'

'Where did you have it last?' said Mum. She sounded cross. 'You promised me that you would only wear it on special occasions.'

Daisy thought hard. 'I remember I had it in the garden yesterday because it clinked against the watering can.'

'Well go and look really hard,' said Mum. 'That bracelet is worth quite a lot of money by now.'

Daisy didn't care about the money, but she did feel bad about breaking her promise, and she really wanted her bracelet back. She searched and searched and searched. The bracelet wasn't on any of the garden paths or on the green grass or on the soil between the flowers in their beds. Daisy sat down on the garden swing feeling tired and sad.

An old woman came through the garden gate and down the path towards her.

'I'll help you find your bracelet, Daisy,' she said. 'You can give me one silver charm in return. Agreed?'

'Oh yes,' said Daisy. 'Agreed.'

'You promise?' said the old lady.

'I really, really promise,' said Daisy.

'Well,' said the old lady, 'I have a clue for you. Here it is.'

Your bracelet is making a Michaelmas daisy chain.

Daisy looked at the paper. It didn't make sense. It was gobbledegook. Meaningless squiggly lines. Then she remembered about mirror writing. She rushed indoors and held the paper towards the mirror in the hall. Immediately seven words sprang into life: *Your bracelet is making a Michaelmas daisy chain.*

How could a bracelet make something? Daisy wondered, but she ran to the part of the garden that had large Michaelmas daisies. Sure enough, there in the centre she saw her bracelet caught between two flower heads. The bracelet was linking the two big daisies, making a daisy chain. It looked like the green stalk of a real daisy chain, only in silver. Daisy snatched it up so eagerly that the head of one of the flowers snapped and hung down sadly from its stalk.

'Now,' said the old lady who had followed Daisy to the Michaelmas daisies. 'Give me one of your charms.'

Daisy looked at each of her charms in turn. She really couldn't bear to part with any of them. *But I must,* she thought. *I did promise.* Daisy thought the old lady looked like a witch in a fairy story, and witches liked cats. Sadly she detached the silver cat from her bracelet. She knew now that the cat had been her favourite charm all along. It had a tail which curled up and over its head and glittery, emerald-green eyes.

I won't give it up, Daisy thought, clutching the cat.

For several long moments, Daisy stood silent and still, holding the small cat in her tightly curled hand. The old lady watched her and waited. Daisy remembered how bad she had felt about breaking her promise to her Mum. Sadly, she unclenched her fist, and reluctantly she handed over her favourite charm.

The old lady nodded her thanks and Daisy watched her walk away down the path and out of the garden. Daisy went back to the swing, sat down and fastened her bracelet around her wrist. She held out her arm and admired it. She moved her wrist. She loved the way the charms tinkled and the way they glinted

as they caught the sun. The little gap where the cat had been spoilt the perfect circle of charms. It left a kind of gap in Daisy's pleasure too. But she had kept her promise, and she had her bracelet back, and she had actually met a witch!

A moment later Daisy's mother came into the garden.

'Tea time, Daisy,' she said. She caught sight of the charm bracelet. 'Ah, you found it,' she exclaimed, sounding pleased. 'Where was it dear?'

'On the Michaelmas Daisies,' Daisy said. 'And I'll put it away now, Mum, and wear it only for best. And, you know what, Mum? A witch helped me to find it.'

'A witch! You've been dreaming, my dear,' said her Mum.

Daisy thought about the old lady dressed in black. Why had she come into the garden anyway? And why did she look a bit like the witch in the story Daisy had been reading? Had she really been a dream?

'I did meet a witch,' she said. 'My little cat has gone. I gave it to her.'

'No one but you has been in the garden,' said her mother.

Daisy couldn't believe this. She didn't want to believe it either. She ran to the Michaelmas daisies. One of them had a broken neck. Its head was hanging on its stem by a thread.

Talking About the Story

Ask the Children

- How had Daisy broken her promise to her Mum?
- How were the Michaelmas daisies **making** a daisy chain?
- What were some of the charms on Daisy's charm bracelet? Which do you think you would like the best? Why?

Points for Discussion

- Did Daisy really meet a witch or was it just a dream? (There is not a right or wrong answer but the children should be able to give good reasons for what they think. It could have been a witch because the clue (mirror writing) was correct and the flower stem really was broken and the little silver cat was gone. It could have been a dream because Mum saw no one come into the garden, Mary has been reading about a witch and where was the piece of paper with the mirror writing?)
- Discuss promises and why we should keep them.
- Can you know that you are not dreaming now? Has anyone ever had a dream that they thought was real?

Cross-curricular Story Activities

Key Stage 1 Activities

1. The children could draw two pictures of Daisy with the old lady, making one picture very realistic and one picture dreamlike. (For example, perhaps in the second picture, the old lady could be more like a storybook witch, and the colours could be more gentle and washy and strange, compared to the realistic, bold colours in a realistic picture.)
2. The children could draw a picture entitled *The Dream*.

Key Stage 2 Activity

The children should write a small piece saying what they believe about this story – was the witch real or a dream? They should give reasons for their answer.

For Enthusiastic and Gifted Children

The children could write and illustrate their own contrasting stories – one in which the witch (or ghost or fairy) is real, and one in which she is not (a dream or a trick of the light, etc.).

Critical Thinking Activities

Key Stage 1 Activities

KS1 Activity 1: Shadows

Give each child a copy of the photograph, Shadow Fish, on page 144 (*Photocopiable Resource 22*). How many fish can they see in the picture? Could some of these only be shadows? Do we sometimes mistake a shadow or a trick of the light for something real?

KS1 Activity 2: Guessing Game

Give the children a copy of the *Photocopiable Resource 23* on page 145. It will be fun for the children to make suggestions about what each of the four images could be. There are no right or wrong answers.

Key Stage 2 Activities

KS2 Activity 1: Ghosts (Alternative Explanations)

Do the children believe in ghosts? Why/why not?

When someone thinks they have seen a ghost, how many alternative (other) explanations can you think of?

KS2 Activity 2: Interpretations

Give the children a copy of the *Photocopiable Resource 23* on page 145. It will be fun for the children to make suggestions about what each of the four images represents. There are no right or wrong answers. The exercise might help them to understand that there is always an element of interpretation in what we see. (Remind the children that we see/interpret the picture in Chapter 2 **as** a rabbit or **as** a duck.)

KS2 Activity 3: An Ambiguous Story

The children could write an ambiguous story about a dream or a ghost. (In other words, as with the story *Daisy Chains*, their story should let the reader decide if something that happens in the story is real or a dream, or if the 'thing' seen is a trick of the light (an illusion), or a real ghost.)

For Enthusiastic or Gifted Children

Just as the fish picture is rather dream-like, they could try to write a dream-like narrative.

Photocopiable Resource 22

Shadow Fish

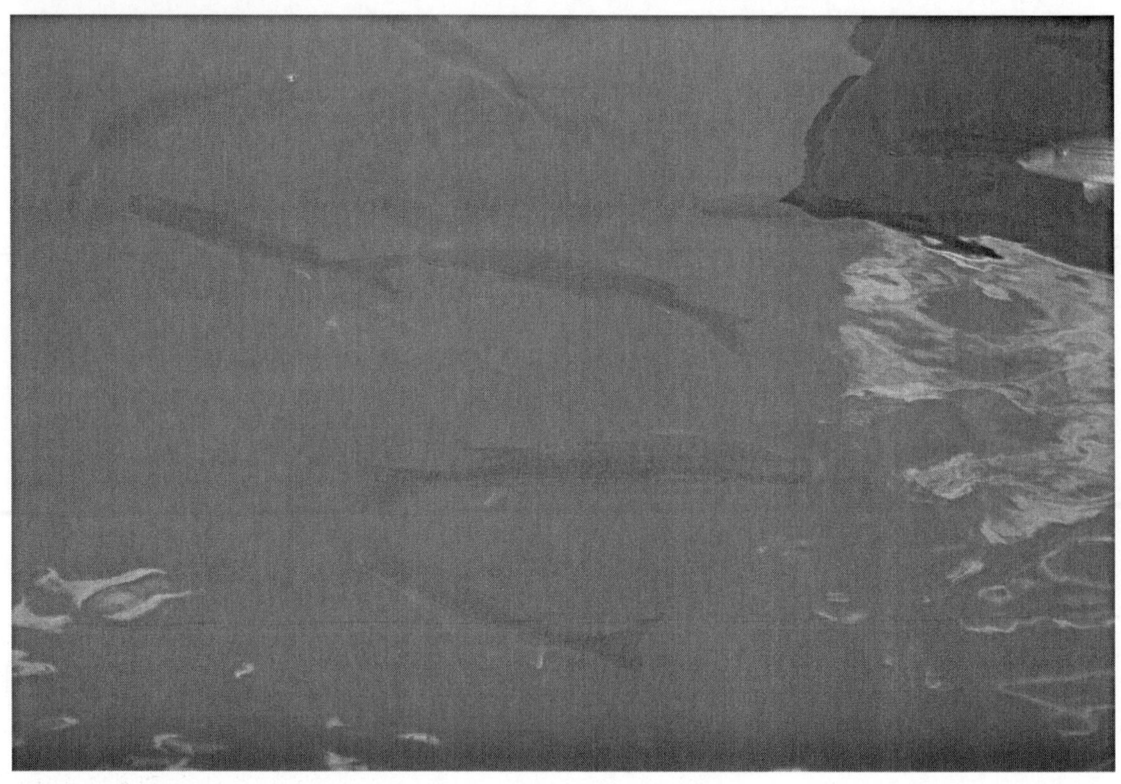

Photocopiable Resource 23

What Do You See?

CHAPTER

Resources

Key Stage One

Fox, E. (2006) *Classroom Tales Using Story Telling to Build Emotional, Social and Academic Skills across the Primary Curriculum*. London: Jessica Kingsley.

Leicester, M. (2006) *Early Years Stories for the Foundation Stage*. London: Routledge.

Moseley, J. (2006) *Quality Circle Time in the Primary Classroom*. Wisbech: LDA.

Moseley, J. and Sonnett, H. (2005) *Here We Go Round: Quality Circle Time for 3–5 Year Olds*. Trowbridge: Positive Press.

Plummer, D. (2005) *The Adventures of the Little Tin Tortoise*. London: Jessica Kingsley.

Key Stage Two

Altiero, J. (2006) *No more Stinking Thinking. A Workbook for Teaching Children Positive Thinking*. London: Jessica Kingsley.

Bowell, T. and Kemp, G. (2002) *Critical Thinking*, 2nd edition. Oxford: Routledge.

Bowkett, S. (2007) *101+ Ideas for Teaching Thinking Skills*. London: Continuum.

Law, S. (2000) *The Philosophy Files*. London: Orion.

Law, S. (2002) *The Philosophy Gym*. London: Orion.

Leicester, M. (2005) *Stories for Circle Time and Assembly*. London: Routledge.

Plummer, D. (2006) *Self Esteem Games for Children*. London: Jessica Kingsley.

Further Reading for Teachers

Brookfield, S. (1987) *Developing Critical Thinking: Challenging Adults to Explore Alternative Ways of Thinking and Acting*. New York: Teachers' College Press.

Department for Children, Schools and Families (2009) *Independent Review of the Primary Curriculum* (Rose Report). London: DCSF.

Epstein, A. S. (2003) How planning and reflection develop young children's thinking skills, *Beyond the Journal: Young Children on the Web*. www.naeyc.org/btj/200309/Planing&Reflection.pdf. (Accessed 22 April 2010.)

Hospers, J. (1956) *An Introduction to Philosophical Analysis*. London: Routledge.

Kolb, D. A. (1984) *Experiential Learning: Experience as a Source of Learning and Development*. Englewood Cliffs, NJ: Prentice-Hall.

Leicester, M. (2010) *Teaching Critical Thinking Skills*. London: Continuum.

Leicester, M. and Taylor, D. (2009) *Environmental Learning for Classroom and Assembly at KS1 and KS2*. London: Routledge.

Macro, C. and McFall, D. (2004) Questions and questioning: working with young children, *Primary Science Review*, 83, May/June: 4–6.

Pascal, C. and Bertram, A. (1997) *Effective Early Learning: Case Studies for Improvement*. London: Hodder & Stoughton.

Thomson, A. (1999) *Critical Reasoning in Ethics: A Practical Introduction*. London: Routledge.